Business Development the Right Way

The CEO Handbook
Volume Two

Dr. Earl R. Smith II

Raven Press

Table of Contents

Introduction

It doesn't matter what business you are in; business development is one of the toughest challenges you have to meet. Your company's future depends on your team's ability to capture an expanding base of clients. Growth is achieved by driving into new markets - expanding business with existing clients - and avoiding serious mistakes that will harm your company's reputation and its ability to get even more business.

~~~~~~~~~~~~~~~~~~~~~~

A central business of business is getting business

~~~~~~~~~~~~~~~~~~~~~~

More energy and effort is put into trying to figure out how to make business development work than any other management function; including advancing the technology that is at the heart of a company's value proposition. There are plenty of books out that that deal with the technologies and tools of business development. This is not one of them. My focus is on the human interactions that accompany the development or expansion of a business development component of your senior management team.

Over the years, I have worked with dozens of CEOs. The

vast majority of them have felt more confident about their company's technology and technological edge than about its ability to generate an expanding customer base. One client put it this way, *"Sure, there is always competition but the core of our management team is focused on delivering advances that keep the company's value proposition ahead of its competition."*

Business development is another thing altogether. Most CEOs that I have worked with have, sooner or later, had a similar experience. Their value proposition was significantly better than the competition's but they still ended up losing the business. In fact, very often the company that is best at business development is well back in the pack then it comes to innovation and cutting edge value propositions. But they win while other companies lose out to them. This is a CEO's worst nightmare. *"We were better than them but we lost out."*

The Constant Challenge

I think back to a program that I organized several years ago. It was focused on the challenges that CEOs of mid-market companies faced. After an introduction, we settled in for a bit of 'brain storming'. The CEOs were asked to 'shout out' brief descriptions of the management challenges they found the most difficult. It was rapid fire. One of the first offered was 'getting business development to work'. That suggestion changed the pattern. I noticed that this challenge was dominating the process. Other CEOs called out variations of it. Some embellished the description. Business development was clearly the eight hundred pound gorilla in the room.

I decided to deal with the big ape and shifted the process to defining the challenge. The group was asked to formulate questions that highlighted it. Here is what they came up with:

o   Why does business development never seem to fully live up to its name?

o   Why is it so difficult to get business development working effectively for my company?

o   Why does my business development team look like a revolving door - with one person after another being hired amid great fanfare only to be let go within a year for 'non-performance'?

o   All these consultants are peddling the same tired old solutions to a problem that never seems to go away. Why can't somebody come up with something that works?

o   The general sentiment was 'there just has to be a better way!'

The experience was not a new one. In my work with CEOs, I've never met one who was really happy with the way business development was working. They all end up saying about the same thing. *"Traditional solutions fail to produce expected results while regularly generating unexpected costs. More and better tools don't seem to make much of a difference. There needs to be a better way."* One particular conversation stands out. It took place in a bar on the upper east side of Manhattan where I had met a fellow CEO for drinks. He had had a particularly frustrating day and was venting big-time.

"Why can't we get this right? It's not complicated and we're supposed to be good at what we do. Why can't we get this damn thing right?" I remember his look of utter frustration. I had started three companies by then and I knew exactly what he was talking about. Being in business begins with getting business. Get it right and you can win big. Get it wrong and nothing else much matters. Business development is one of the major challenges that every CEO and senior team must meet and master.

For all my experience, I had little to suggest to my frustrated companion. It was a very humbling experience and I realized that I had been carrying the same burden. All CEOs face the same challenge.

My frustration grew until there was no way out but to find an alternative approach that really worked. Finding a way to make business development work became a crusade. After we parted, my walk up First Avenue towards my home on East 59th Street in Manhattan became the first steps on that quest.

My fourth company showed me the way forward. Six months after my dismal performance in the bar I had the beginnings of a solution. Those first insights formed the core of an innovative, potent and cost-effective approach to business development.

Much of the last two decades has been spent developing then refining a solution to what I see as the principal point of pain for most CEOs. During that time I was guided by three goals.

- First, the solution had to be head-and-shoulders better than competing strategies
- Second, it had to be highly cost effective – minimizing the drain on critical resources while generating maximum benefits in the form of turbo-charged business development
- And third, it had to work!

A New Approach

The second half of *Business Development the Right Way* describes how an advisory board populated with highly experienced, committed and well-connected individuals can be the most effective way to drive a company's growth. This book describes the design, operation and management of boards that will radically increase the effectiveness of your company's business development process.

Business Development the Right Way shows you how it is done and, more importantly, that it can be done for virtually any company. Its core messages are:

o   Getting business development right is one of the primary challenges for any senior team,
o   There is a solution to this persistent and painful challenge,
o   The solution is potent and cost effective and,
o   Given a professional approach, this solution can be deployed for virtually any company.

Business Development the Right Way shows you how a well-run business development team coupled with an advisory board, properly structured and populated by highly influential, committed and well-connected individuals can drive a company's revenue. In this book I describe the design, population and management of these boards and show how they can increase the effectiveness of a company's business development process.

Mentoring As a Bonus

"Once we launched the board, I realized that none of my senior team had ever had a true mentor. I realized that I had never had one either. Now we all have very experienced people working with us; helping us to perfect our craft. That alone is worth the price of the board. The increased business is almost just a bonus"

That was one CEO's comment on the impact of a board I had built for her company. Modern corporate culture does not foster mentoring relationships as effectively as traditional ones used to. With my advisory boards these mentoring relationships naturally develop. CEOs and senior team members now are not in it alone. There are very experienced people that they trust who are providing advice and guidance. In many cases these mentoring relationships are life changing.

The material for the book has been drawn from experiences with dozens of C-level executives, consultants and members of boards of directors and advisory boards. The goal of the book is to help you understand how to build an effective business development team and the value proposition behind advisory boards as business development engines.

About Me

I have been mentoring senior executives and corporations for more than two decades. I got into mentoring after a successful career as a recidivist entrepreneur. I founded and built six companies. The experience of building those businesses brought many good times but I have recently been thinking about all those clients I mentored and the successes that they have had. Some of my fondest memories have resulted from those mentoring engagements.

Over the years, I have provided executive mentoring, leadership guidance, organizational support, team and life mentoring. Each is different but the focus has always been the same – working to help my clients unlock their potential and enjoy successes that they never thought possible.

I provide mentoring to those who have both the courage and determination to make a truly transformational journey. My approach is heavily influenced by core principles of Zen Buddhism. I don't offer quick fixes or follow the latest fads. If you are willing to make the long journey – if it's time for you to come to know the person you really are and can become – if you intend to finally find the path you should be following – if you want to start living life you were truly meant to live – then perhaps we should talk. Send me an e-mail and we'll arrange a time to chat.

Dr. Earl R. Smith II
Washington, DC
March 2014
DrSmith@Dr-Smith.com

Business Development

Business Development Should Live Up To Its Name

In the spirit of disclosure, I am a recidivist entrepreneur who has developed a unique approach to business development. My approach involves:

o   a careful approach to building and managing a business development team;
o   a board of advisers, which is populated by very senior people who are dedicated to driving the top line;
o   a different approach to resourcing and organizing a company's senior management team; and
o   an approach that focuses on building revenue in larger chunks.

Start with the Business Development Team

One of the most difficult challenges that a CEO of a small to medium-sized company faces is the development and management of an effective business development effort. A major part of this challenge is knowing when and how to start building a business development team. Early on the founder's vision, contacts and personal resources drive a company's revenue. At some point, the resources and contacts become insufficient to sustain growth at high levels. The company establishes a business development group, and, in doing so, gives birth to what often becomes a major source of frustration, wasted time and resources.

Business development becomes an add-on to the principal organization and function of a company. It adds a new type of employee to the team; an individual who specialize in identifying and capturing new business rather than in the core skill sets that have built the company. They are often among the first 'outsiders' that a corporate culture experiences.

This 'outsider' status creates all sorts of problems. Cliques tend to form and tensions rise between those who are focused on technology and those who are focused on growing the business. Organizational dysfunctionality is quite common. This can, and often does, lead to increasing internal frictions that degrade a company's performance. Once such a dynamic sets in, it quickly becomes apparent to interested parties like customers and suppliers. In the extreme it can end up 'branding' the company as dysfunctional. This is a tough reputation to overcome once it sets in.

Although many CEOs tend to think that this is a problem specific to their company, it is one of the most common results of success. Once the company begins to grow, the senior management team needs to know a lot more about how to manage the business effectively. They become more and more focused on the business of business rather than the business of the business. This requires them, among a raft of other things, to develop and deploy a professional and effective business development strategy. The problem comes as the CEO and members of the senior team react to this need. They may see 'selling' as beneath them or may simply not be very good at business development.

One CEO I worked with started out as a programmer - a 'code monkey' as he called it. As such, his life was mostly in a cubicle front of a computer screen. He had developed a range of anti-social tendencies which made it difficult for him to interact with decision makers at potential clients. They found him aloof and dismissive. He thought of them as shallow and wasting his time. You can imagine how productive most of the meetings, and his attempts at business development, were.

Making the Turn

No matter how the crisis evolves, there is only one way forward. Management must find a way to meet the business development challenge. The judgment of their success or failure is unforgiving. If they succeed, the company will grow, more jobs will be created and they will be richly compensated. If they fail, none of that will occur. Two futures confront every management team. In order to realize that brighter future, business development must be made to live up to its name and purpose.

My own attempts to grapple with that challenge lead me to develop a disciplined approach to standing up a business development team as well as advisory boards that were focused on business development. As years and experience have contributed to the concept, business development has become their predominate purpose. Like horses that have been bred for speed, these advisory boards know how to run faster than the competition. That's what they do - they burn up the track.

But, to take my equine example a bit further, a thoroughbred requires the right jockey in order to shine. An advisory board requires a management team that can harvest the value it brings. For the right company and with the right approach an advisory board dedicated to driving the revenue line can be a highly effective and extremely cost effective alternative approach to business development. It is the correct pairing that makes it work.

So how do you determine if yours is one of the 'right' companies? I have spent a lot of time on this question. Here are a few questions that might help you decide:

o   Have you had enough with the costs and results of traditional approaches?

o   You are seriously ready to try something different?

o   Is your management team composed of mature, experienced people who know their business?

o   Is your company providing mature products or services to a broad base of clients?

o   Do you have a run rate rather than a burn rate?

o   Does your management team deal well with change?

If this sounds like you and your company, then you are probably a good candidate for an advisory board focused on driving revenue growth. But before you pick up the phone and ask a bunch of your friends to be on your board, read this book. It can help you avoid embarrassment and show you how it should be done.

You might think that designing, building and managing such a combination is easy. I'm here to tell you that it is a subtle and demanding challenge. Get it right and you will have to run hard to keep up. Get it wrong and you will waste a lot of time and treasure.

One thing I have learned about designing and structuring these teams and boards; it is a bad idea for a management team to undertake such a journey without supervision and lots of support. They are intended to be very powerful assets. Concentrating such levels of power can threaten some of your team members. I have seen teams attempt to 'de-fang' the process by choosing 'safe and cuddly' board members. A pre-emptive effort at protection of the status quo that results in a completely ineffective board.

The results of this approach can be startlingly effective. An advisory board populated with very senior individuals who have established themselves as centers of influence, when supported by the right business development team, can open important doors and provide important endorsements. It can move a company to a whole new level.

A well designed and populated board is a challenge for management. Dealing with such a board is a very demanding experience. Lots of your team's approaches to doing business will be challenged. They will find themselves needing to up their game in the face of superior knowledge and experience. The pace quickens and becomes more purposeful.

Starting on this journey is easier than staying the course. Not starting is easier than both. But the path from 'here to the next level' is through a gauntlet of gut checks, self-examinations and evolutionary leaps. Success brings not only a more robust run rate; it also brings a superior management team ready to manage a company that has successfully made the leap to the next level.

Potholes, Pitfalls, Reefs and Dead Ends

The landscape of most corporations is littered with the remains, scars and war stories of filled attempts at making business development work. When I do preliminary diligence for an engagement, I focus on the company's history. It is helpful to know the paths that management followed to get the company to where is currently is. One of the things that most often stands out is the instability in the business development team. A second is the distancing between that part of the team and the rest.

A company embarks on its first attempts to establish a distinct business development under pressure to continue expansion and following a 'logical imperative'. The combination of these two can create opportunities for a very rough ride.

Pressure

There is an old saying, 'success has many parents but failure is an orphan.' Such simple minded formulations overlook the fact that success brings opportunities for even more spectacular failures. Pressure to expand business development efforts generally comes from past successes. But it also comes from a realization that the 'old way' of driving the top line is increasingly inadequate if the growth rate of the prior years is going to be maintained.

This realization strikes hard at the core of the self-images of the senior management team. If the claim of both omnipotence and omniscience has not flowered into hubris, it certainly has become the foundation of confidence; and, perhaps, pride. Senior team members, who have in the past, lead the way find themselves unable to 'keep up the pace'. It is hard to overstate the impact of this realization. It strikes at the very heart of most CEO's self-image. Potholes, which challenge the confidence of senior team members, begin to show up in the road ahead. This challenge to confidence has a ripple effect. It moves through the team and can begin to affect the company's public image.

Pitfalls

The first response to this pressure is predictable. Management tries to soldier on. They put more energy into business development the old way. Two things happen as a result. The first is they take their eyes off of managing the company. There are only so many hours in the day and time spent focusing on business development is time not available for other areas. The second is a diminishing return on time spent doing business development.

A good way to think of this is as a multiple-stage rocket. The first stage is designed to get the whole thing off the ground. After its job is done, the second stage takes over. Is it reasonable, after it has spent its fuel, to expect the first stage to continue driving the rocket higher?

At some point it becomes clear that this first strategy is not working well enough. That is where the first pitfall appears. Management feels that they have failed in some way. They need to find others to do successfully what they have less and less been able to deliver on. They know that the company needs to grow and that that means bringing in more business. They also know that the chunks of business won need to get larger. Chasing lots of smaller pieces is no longer 'feeding the bear'.

And so senior management decides to follow what they see as a logical imperative. 'Let's find some business development types and bring them onto the team.' Most often, the first step they take dooms the entire effort to failure. The go searching for people to interview. Some companies begin to search the job boards while others employ search consultants. The result is often the same.

Reefs

Management begins to interview for a position that it has not completely defined nor understood. It also lacks an understanding of the metrics that should be used to evaluate candidates. But there is a more basic reason why this process is fraught with dangers. They are interviewing a type of person who is very different from most, if not all, of their team members.

The best way to come to terms with why this is true is to consider the nature of the people being interviewed. Business development types exist in a parallel universe to the one that management occupies. The 'laws of relationships' are different in that parallel universe. For one thing, they are much more focused on the welfare of the individual. Business development people tend to be outriders who join teams for purely instrumental reasons. Like an wandering atheist who joins the church offering the most advantages, business development professionals tend to move from company to company seeking advantages.

A second characteristic of business development types is that they are very good at presenting themselves in ways that overcome potential obstacles to achieving their goals. This ability is never in sharper operation than when they are being interviewed for a new gig. They are better at being interviewed than the people on the other side of the table are at interviewing. In a battle of wits, one side is less well prepared.

The result of this process is almost always unsatisfactory to all sides. The business development professional gets a job and may keep it for a year or so. But production falls short of expectations and, at some point, excuses begin to replace promises. Management's ride is no smoother. After congratulating themselves on a good hire, they sit back and wait for the new business to come rolling in. Of course, it doesn't.

If you really want to see the footprints of this process, glace through the resumes that you receive when you set out to recruit a new business development team member. What you will see is a series of jobs which lasted a year to eighteen months.

So, six to nine months into the arrangement the CEO begins to wonder if the right person is leading the business development charge. Existing clients are wondering the same thing. Close to that time the team member begins to realize that things are not going according to plan and starts quietly look around for the next gig.

It doesn't have to be that way.

Why Is Business Development So Difficult To Get Right

Every conversation I have with a CEO eventually touches on the same question - '*How does my company get traction in new markets with new clients?*' This challenge seems to rank right up there with arranging adequate financial resources and recruiting and retaining top people.

This challenge often did not limit growth in the early stages. During that time, the contacts and reputation of the founders and key executives drove the 'top line'. Most often the client base came to resemble a silo in a corn field with one client dominating the business mix surrounded by other smaller ones that represented stunted attempts at broadening the base.

To be sure, this start up strategy is one of the preferred ways of launching a company. It is an indicator that the management team has any business at all starting the business. If they don't have ready clients for their product of service, they should get them before going forward.

But why, once the initial growth phase is over, is it so difficult to keep business development going? Why do the business development slots look so much like revolving doors? And, why is it that growing a company from nil to ten or fifteen million in annual revenues often does not seem to prepare management to take it to thirty or fifty million?

Reason One: The senior management (particularly the CEO) is not really committed to making the journey. This is more common than you might think. Corporate growth requires significant self-reinvention among key members of the senior team. Often they are not prepared to give up control or manage a larger operation. Some prefer 'writing code' or whatever the company's principal business happens to be. But whatever their 'rationale', they don't want to or can't become managers. In this case, expenditures on business development can just be a waste of resources. Better save the money and buy the new car.

Reason Two: The organizational structure pretty much guarantees failure. Business development is often an afterthought add-on to the organizational structure. It operates in a quasi-independent status with loose reporting arrangements to the CEO or COO. This can create major problems. Business development should be integral to the company's organizational structure and the CEO needs to be the senior business development member of the team. I once attended an all-hands retreat of a company where the COO gave the business development report. That spoke volumes on how the company saw the three business development employees standing in the wings. They were, of course, replaced by newer models by the next retreat and the revolving door was kept in good working order.

Reason Three: Business development is seen as the province of middle-level people. Think of the message that such an approach gives potential new clients. *"Talk to the 'lessers' and, if we deem you worthy, we will let you talk to the senior people."* New clients of mid-range companies need/want to see the top person early in the process. It is the CEO that represents the company's commitment to client satisfaction, the ability of the company to commit as well as the ability of the client to find some person to rely on. Each time a decision-maker chooses to go with a new company they take a huge risk. If it goes wrong, how much faith do you think such a person would put in a middle level person with no real connection to the company's culture?

Reason Four: The wrong people for the job: A company often will bring in 'business development' types as a first attempt to attack the problem of widening the client base. These people are 'specialists' in chasing business but frequently not specialists in the business of the company. Most often they are walled-off from the company's principal clients and are limited to higher risk, longer cycle targets. This approach can resource-starve functions that a company needs to work in order to successfully grow its top line. For example, money is spent on business development types while the proposal development, capture and red-teaming are radically under-resourced.

Reason Five: What is all this making us look like in the market place? It's called branding; establishing the reputation of the company in the minds of actual and potential customers. It can be the least understood and most dangerous threat to any company's future. How is your company known? What is its reputation? How well do you understand why customers do business with you? Are you known as a group that knows how business is done? Or are you branded as a company that has 'out-sourced' its future? These 'costs' are often overlooked as being less important than the business of the business. This mistake has probably killed more companies than any other. How you are known determines how seriously you are taken; and that largely determines what opportunities you will see and how successful you will become.

There are more reasons than these five but I suspect that you are getting the idea. Business development is a tough nut to crack for any management team. There are more dead bodies in that field than live travelers. Without careful planning and disciplined execution, the results are likely to be both disappointing and frustrating.

Business Development and Failure to Launch

One of the major challenges that a CEO faces comes when it becomes necessary to build a business development capability beyond that of the core operating team. The challenge reemerges when that capability needs to be expanded. In fact, it is one of the most regularly recurring challenges. More of that later. But, for now, let's start with the first time.

Your company has become increasingly profitable. It has an expanding business base, a growing reputation for quality and reliability and a culture that seems to please most of your team most of the time.

But there is a cloud on the horizon. You know that the team is doing its best to bring in business. They are always on the lookout for opportunities to expand the beachheads that you have helped them establish. The problem is that it is looking more and more like you are going to harvest all that there is from that process. You need to build the capability of reaching new clients and capturing new business.

Something else has been bothering you. Your financial statements are telling you that the cost of targeting, pursuing, capturing and then delivering on those smaller chunks of business is getting to be more than the profit margins you expected. Clearly you need to start winning bigger chunks.

The Fateful Decision

Like most CEOs, you decide that it is time to bring in people who specialize in business development. You and your team have been doing it all along but now it is time to get some fulltime 'professionals' on it. So maybe you start with the job boards or your network. Maybe you contact a recruiter. Either way, the word gets out that you are hiring.

You end up getting a stack of resumes right off the bat. As the word gets around that you are hiring, that stack turns into a flood.

They come in all sizes and level of details. Now you are stuck. You are looking through a series of resumes in an attempt to fill a new position and you know neither the applicants nor the real functioning of the position. Sure you can say "I want you to go out and get new business - and bring in bigger chunks" but that is hardly an understanding.

In desperation you attempt to get other members of your team involved. Maybe your assistant becomes the first screen for the resumes. You give some guidance - look for experience related to our business, no jumpers (people who seem to change jobs every year or so), nobody with less than three year's experience, etc. Your assistant begins sorting out the survivors and soon you have a neat pile of resumes on your desk; all of which passed your screens.

Let the Parade Begin

This is may be your first experiences with a more formal process of identifying, vetting and negotiating with potential team members. During the initial interviews you meet all the usual characters including some of these:

o   The one meeting wonder: These people are great at first meetings but turn out to be the proverbial one trick pony. The first meeting goes well and then they turn into some sort of antisocial hunchback. You get your first signal when the follow up communication from them is either obviously canned or makes a reference that makes no sense. At the University of Texas we used to refer to these people as 'all hat and no cattle'.

o   The 'elevator speech masters': With these types, the good times don't even last through the first meeting. They are the proverbial mile wide and inch deep. With their ego in full flower, you are assaulted with a steady stream of self-aggrandizing drivel that more civilized people call bragging but I tag as public masturbation. The real problem with these 'elevator speech' types is that they neither know nor care about you or your company. The interview is 'their time to shine'. They just want a paycheck.

o   Miscreants: "*You do know that this is an interview for a senior position with a company that is in the business of serving professional clients?*" That was the question that one of my clients put to a candidate who arrived half an hour late for the interview and was dressed like one of the village people. Another favorite are candidates who seem to think that an interview is a 'mine's bigger than yours' type of contest. I had one tell me that he knew better how to run my business than I did. He seemed confused when I ended the interview by wishing him well in competing with us and adding that I was uncomfortable discussing the inner workings of my company with a potential competitor.

o   The Avatars: Welcome to the post-modernist world. You get a resume that seems too good to be true and schedule an interview. The resume sits on your desk while the time approaches when you may finally meet the business development professional of your dreams. You scan it on occasion. You even do a bit of Goggling and visit the websites of the companies they have worked for. Then the person arrives. After the first ten minutes you want to ask them when the person who is described in the resume is going to show up.

Well, you get the idea and, if you have been down that road, you have probably been shaking your head as the memories flood back.

You discuss the process with your team and some of them express reservations about having this new person chase business with existing clients. This concern is partially out of self-interest (they get compensated when they bring in new business) and partially out of concern for the company and its reputation. After all, this new person is not as steeped in the company's value proposition as the others are.

Your CFO is telling you that this person will be all overhead - 0% billable. That is going to be a big change from how business development has been funded.

Your COO is not sure about this move at all. Who will this person report to? Are they part of his span of control or do they report directly to you? Does that mean that business development is split with part of it going through her and part directly to you?

The closer you get to actually making a hire, the more complicated things seem to be.

References

So maybe you have it narrowed down to four or six candidates by now. All have passed the initial interview and survived follow-on ones with your senior team. And during that process you have requested and received references from each candidate. If you've done it the traditional way (that is to say the wrong way) you have called those people who were offered as references. Low and behold, all of them had very positive things to say. And then maybe you resorted to a cheap trick like 'give me somebody who doesn't like you'.

Of course, the right way is to identify those positions which the candidate has filled in the past that most closely resemble the one you are seeking to fill and ask for supervisors and CEOs as references. In other words, you pick the references.

Either way you end up talking to a series of people you probably don't know. In each case you have a few minutes to gather what information you can. But you suffer the disadvantage of not knowing the person on the other end of the line. And you know little of their agenda. (I once heard a CEO gleefully tell how he was more than glad to give a good report on past employees that were real 'screw ups' if the company they were going to work for was, in any way, a competitor)

References can be helpful but you need to stay out of the traditional channels and break into a different approach.

Then It Begins

But let's say that you soldier on and pick a candidate. You make an offer, which is accepted, and schedule a meeting to clean up the details. As a polite host, you want the candidate to ask questions. You have a few of your own. You want to know how soon your investment is going to pay off. What business is going to be pursued initially? But there are also concerns that you need to express. For instance, you reveal that you will wall off the existing client base.

The meeting goes well until you start asking your questions. Then things get a little out of focus. You (unreasonably) are expecting specific answers and firm assurances. That is not what you are getting.

Traditionalists and Futurists

I sometimes work with companies that are on the verge of leaving what I call the 'village stage'. They are pushing into the great uncertainty of corporate adolescence. This push, and the stress which accompanies it, is one of the seminal periods in the development of any company. By the time I arrive on the scene, the battle lines often have been well formed and the organization has divided into two camps. The coming battle will present severe challenges for the founders, senior team and the company. The prevailing camp will get to decide what the future will hold for all involved.

Let me start by defining what I mean by 'village stage'. First off, defining a company in terms of its gross revenue is not useful. I've seen organizations generating close to twenty million dollars in gross revenue while still operating within this paradigm. Secondly, the size of the organization in terms of its client base or human resources is also not a good indicator. I have encountered companies with twenty to thirty major clients and over a hundred employees that are still operating as a cottage business. Finally, the age of a company is an unreliable indicator as well. Once a company slips into what I call 'life-style mode' it enters a period of repressed adolescence that can last through its entire life span.

There are a number of indicators which are very useful in identifying a company which is still operating within the 'village' paradigm and facing the complex issues of reinventing itself. The most notable of them are: the evolving nature of leadership, the changing nature of employees, the definition of span of control, the performance and behavior of the founders, the level of professionalism within the corporate culture and the ability of the company to allow its culture to evolve in order to cope with the increasing burdens that always accompany rapid growth and increased size.

At the core of this battle is a conflict between the traditionalists and futurists. The traditionalists are generally those who have been with the company for a long time. They have gotten used to the way things have been done and like it that way. They are within their comfort zone. On the other side are the futurists. These are generally newer team members who have been brought on to help take the company to the next level. They are not comfortable with the way things are and are determined to shake things up. The battle is over the vision for the future of the company.

The Evolving Nature of leadership: In the village stage, leadership tends to be defined by the traditionalist. For many, because of their own rather limited management experience, their vision of leadership tends to be based on position and prerogative rather than inspiration and example.

As a company grows, it comes under increasing pressure to bring in more experienced managers. These newcomers tend to pose an immediate threat to the prevailing theory of leadership. In a sense a new coin of the realm begins circulate and to compete with the old currency. Employees now face a choice that wasn't available earlier on. On the one hand there are the traditionalists who may continue to insist that they are the leaders and should be followed without question. On the other there are futurists who bring new, and often very creative, approaches to defining leadership. Their leadership is based on the proposition of 'do as I do' rather than 'do as I say'. They lead by example.

Traditionalists are the ones most challenged by this evolution in the operative concept of leadership. It takes an exceptional person to give up the security of the '*I own the business so you will do as I say*' attitude in favor of the more risky and challenging '*follow me when I need to lead and I will follow you when it is better that you lead*'. How the traditionalists react to this option has a major impact on the future of the company.

The Changing Nature of Employees: As an organization grows, and the pressures to generate higher performance increase, employees will seek out leadership and form allegiances which will empower them to meet new, and far more difficult, challenges. The futurists will have experience and skill sets that are often not present among the futurists. Some of them will take leadership roles in areas that have traditionally been the prerogative of the old team. This always results in tensions that are felt company-wide.

Over time, two camps evolve within the company. The first tends to find these changes unsettling. They often wistfully reminisce about the good old days when the company was more like a family than a business. They are bound together by a network of relationships, some of which are deeply personal. Their approach to the business tends to be conservative and focused on 'growing without major changes in the corporate culture'. As the battle approaches they will often adopt a Fort Apache the Bronx approach; circling the wagons and defending what they consider to be the pure heart and soul of the company.

On the other side of this developing divide is the new breed of employee whose vision of the company generally extends farther into the future. Their vision involves not only substantial continued growth but an increasingly professionalized environment which includes a professionalization of the management team and a significant and sustained evolution of the corporate culture. These employees tend to lack the emotional connection to the traditionalists comfort zone. They've signed on not because they are true believers in the traditionalists but were attracted to the opportunities that the company has now become able to offer.

The Definition of Span of Control: One of the early indicators of the coming battle is a widening disagreement over the concept of span of control. In traditional, modernist management terms span of control is defined in terms of a list of those individuals who report directly to a given person. This 'post Fordist' vision is the most common one adopted by traditionalists because, in the early stages, all roads lead to them. But this vision of an organization is fundamentally flawed.

In truth this rather basic version only works in the most primitive of organizational structures; when leadership is based upon prerogative and position. But things get considerably more complicated as the company's operations expand. Informal reporting patterns begin to evolve based upon perceived competence and charisma rather than prerogative and position.

Inevitably informal networks develop. Employees develop strong relationships with individuals they trust and respect and who relate to them in a supportive and empowering way. Pressures build when there is an increasing divergence between these informal and formal relationships.

The Performance and Behavior of the Traditionalists: In the early stages of a company's growth most founders tend to fancy themselves as 'chief-of-everything'. They have 'final say' on virtually everything that affects the company. Few things are minor enough to escape their attention. But as the company grows this becomes a practical impossibility. (Although I have known founders who have given the impossible a heroic and generally destructive shot.)

In purely human terms there becomes too much to

31

understand and process – too many skills to master – too many places and people to be – for the traditionalist clique to remain master of everything. Additionally the challenges that a company faces as it grows become both more complex and specialized. Solutions require extensive knowledge and experience in skill areas, very often skill sets that the traditionalist often do not have.

If the traditionalists try to maintain their control, the company will be limited to the size that this management approach allows. It will grow until the internal pressures threaten to cause an implosion. Most often, traditionalists who cannot bring themselves to let go and delegate will (sometimes unconsciously) work to keep the company a 'manageable size'.

But if the traditionalists successfully reinvent themselves, the team will expand to include new members with more sophisticated knowledge in important areas. The futurists will take the lead.

The Level of Professionalism within the Corporate Culture: When founders start out to build a company, there are many areas where they are just 'making it up as they go along'. Many of these are in the 'non-technology' parts of the business of growing a business. Finances can be managed out of the proverbial cigar box. Human resources is handled by visits to job boards or word-of-mouth searches. Decisions about which business opportunities to pursue are generally made opportunistically and with an eye towards survival. Little attention tends to be paid to the definition and evolution of a corporate culture and the attention that is paid tends to be superficial.

There is some point in the evolution of every company that marks the beginning of the end of the viability of these kinds of 'off-the-cuff' strategies. They just don't seem to be working like the used to. Things get more complex and the need to be supported by systems that are robust and effective. The impact of the failure tends to increase and the traditionalists spend more and more time crisis managing.

Professionalization of the team means bringing in new members who have deeper knowledge and experience in the process of running a company (and often less in the technology, product or service that is the company's foundation). Some major areas of professionalization that can cause internal stress are: proposal development and delivery, capture, red-teaming, sales, human resources, financial control and general management. That these new skill sets are critical to the growth of any company is not the question. How a company deals with meeting or avoiding these needs is.

The Ability of the Company to Allow Its Culture to Evolve: An adult will do poorly in most civilized societies if they have repressed the process of maturing and are still acting like a child. The same is true of a company and its culture. Growth means change but it also means evolution along well defined pathways.

There are two broad paths that present themselves to a company moving out of the village stage and into adolescence. One road takes it towards what I call a 'life-style' company, one which meets primarily the needs of the traditionalists leaving the rest of the team to decide whether their needs are being fulfilled. Along this road, employees have to accommodate the circumstances desired by the traditionalists or leave in search of greener pastures. If the traditionalists prevail, many of the best often do.

The second road opens towards growth beyond expectations and focuses on meeting the needs of an expanding team. This option requires the traditionalists to evolve in ways that allow them to help the expanding team meet their needs. If they cannot evolve in these ways, they need to leave the team.

Corporate culture must evolve and become more adult-like if a company's growth is going to be sustainable. The issue becomes whether it is going to have the chance to grow and realize its potential.

The Ten Percenters: So how does a company decide between the paths of repressed adolescence on the one hand and maturing on the other? You probably noticed that I have made extensive references to the role and impact of the attitudes and capacities of the traditionalists so it will come as no surprise that I believe, at least initially, the future of the company is in their hands. The truth is that they make the first choices. They must choose a path out of the village. These choices are often best if they allow others to participate. Even so, these first steps are only the initial skirmishes in the battle.

I have seen these battles rage on for years with both sides struggling for supremacy. During this time massive amounts of damage accrue. I have watched traditionalists, in reaction to perceived challenges to their supremacy, resort to the nuclear option and become true dictators in their own house. In those cases the results have always been disastrous.

At other times one or more of them accomplishes an evolutionary leap. They reinvent themselves to a new type of leader and put the status of traditionalist on the shelf. Here progress is made and, over time, the battle may get resolved productively.

On more than one occasion I have seen the newer, more professional team members get fed up and go off on their own. They simply leave the village to the traditionalists. That result puts the company back to square one in the process and the battle lines tend to reform anew as different futurists are brought onboard.

These battles rage on as long as issues such as the ones described above are potent and until one or the other side abandons the field. Two roads diverge in a leafy wood and the company can only take one. One leads to limits and eternal adolescence until death - the other to a path to healthy adulthood. The future is in the hands of the traditionalists and the outlook is not rosy. My experience has been that, by their actions, rather than their words, seven out of ten of these groups drive their company towards the first and downward path.

Sales, Marketing and Business Development

When you set about to build a business development team, one of the most confounding challenges is to balance a group of functions that accompany it. Certainly, there are support services like finance, accounting and human relationships that need to be balanced. Your experience as a CEO will help you meet and master these challenges. I am talking about the more closely related functions of sales and marketing. Many CEOs have difficulty sorting out these related disciplines and understanding just how they fit together.

One of the major challenges that you face is understanding the differences between sales, marketing and business development. This is the source of serious challenges and misunderstandings that can have costly consequences.

Good sales people are diamonds that should be collected, supported and nurtured. That being said, they are relatively straight forward folk whose work ethic is directly connected to their success. It's fairly easy to develop performance metrics for sales people. You give them a quota that they work to meet. If they meet it, both you and they are happy. If they don't, then there is trouble in the house. Sales people seldom make good business development team members and they are almost always terrible at marketing.

One of the major reasons that this is true rests upon the principal characteristic of any top-flight sales person - they are impatient and always focused on the 'kill'. Sales people are true hunters. They stalk their quarry as if it were prey and constantly think about how to best move in for the kill. Most of the very good sales people I have worked with have little patience for long term planning or strategy. They are tightly focused on the near term and how it will affect their chances to earn more this year than the year before.

Maybe a wild west example might help. Sales people are like bounty hunters. You give them a poster and they head out with every intent to capture the 'bad guy' and bring him back to jail. The bounty hunter thinks is terms of locating, capturing and incarcerating the target. They use a highly developed intelligence network in the search and get very focused when the target has been identified.

Business development types are more like sheriffs. They take the longer, community view of their role. The sheriff meets with the mayor and town council. The job includes keeping the peace, enforcing the laws and working for the better future of the town. Sheriffs are more prone to long-term planning and strategic thinking. Sure, they sometimes act like bounty hunters but they are generally more the 'let's organize a posse and track them down' types.

Like the sheriff, good business development types are focused on an extended process; one that runs from the branding of the company, through the targeting proposal development and capture phases and into the company's future.

It is not as easy to develop metrics for business development types but it can be done. The most logical starting point is the pipeline and the velocity of targets moving through it. If sales people are good at closing the deal, business development people are good as setting the conditions that make the closing of the deal more likely. They have a longer-term vision of the process and develop a wider range of relationships.

If sales people are bounty hunters and business development types are sheriffs, marketing specialists are the 'women's temperance society' of the town. In the mid-market, government contractor space, this is generally the last function to be added during a growth surge and the first one to be eliminated during a downsizing. Marketing is the 'civilizing' influence within a growing company. Its focus is heavily on branding and the reputation of the company, the attractiveness of core value propositions and the coherence of the company's image.

As a result of this focus, it is relatively more difficult to come up with effective metrics for marketing people. Since they are seldom directly connected with revenue generation (that being filtered through the business development and sales teams), performance expectations are more difficult to set.

A friend of mine summed all of this up nicely. "When I send a sales person out I expect a dead mammoth nearly every time. When I send a business development type on the same journey, I expect a mammoth about half of the time and a description of how the mammoth got away the other half. Now with marketing, I never expect a mammoth. Mostly I get a description of the nice glade of trees that the mammoth herd was lounging in. Sales people accept responsibility for failure and feel shame. Business development people offer excuses and stories about how the target just slipped away but I suspect that they also feel shame - but maybe not as much. Marketing types tend to attribute failure to the poor implementation of other members of the team. They don't seem to feel shame - only frustration."

Well, that is admittedly only one view of sales, business development and marketing but it should give you some idea of how intricate the interrelationships are and how difficult it can be to balance them. It is important to always keep clearly in focus the fact that standing up a business development function is never a free-standing project. Normal functions of the company need to evolve and strengthen while other skill sets have to be developed. Nothing about the process is straight forward.

Building a Business Development Team the Right Way

So here is the situation as we face it. "Your company embarks on its first attempts to establish a distinct business development .." But now, let's imagine that you and your senior team decides do something out of pattern; you decide to bring in someone who has successfully built a business development team before.

To be clear, I am not talking about a senior business development team member. In this case, you and I open discussions. I am not someone who is interested in joining your team but has successfully built teams in the past. If you select the right advisor, the process will be far different than you expect - and far more productive. Let's assume for the purposes of what follows, that I am that person.

My first meeting with you generally involves a refocusing of the agenda. Your presumption may be that your company is ready to build a business development team and only needs to 'find the right people'. If we can't get by that assumption, there is little need to extend conversations. The fact is that there is a lot of spade work that needs to be done before the recruitment process can be kicked into gear. Companies that don't do this preparation are gambling with the company's future rather than building it.

It is rare that anything other than frustration comes out of such a first meeting. You and your senior team have a burr under your saddles and are ready to have it seen to. One potential client actually said to me, "screw this getting ready stuff, I am a doer, let's get going and doing." Needless to say that meeting did not end up well. However, a year later and after the revolving door had made a couple of quick turns, he was back and in a more reasonable mood.

The core challenge in the beginning is to approach the question of building an expanded business development capability in the same way that best practices dictate approaching any strategic initiative. First you analyze - then you plan - then you red-team -

and then you implement. My best engagements get through the initial frustrations quickly and move on to organizing that planning process.

Analyze

The first step is to get a very clear picture of the history and current business base of the company. We need to carefully build that picture; no shortcuts please. "Of course, we understand", is not going to cut it. Every time I've helped a team work through the process they end up realizing that they did not 'understand' clearly enough.

The first phase is focused on building that clear understanding. We go through the delivery history, the developed quals, the dead ends, the business that has expanded, the missteps, the business won and the business lost, the profitable and unprofitable contracts (one company that did this discovered that half of their run rate was under water - they were losing money on that business). We also test the reporting process to verify that the numbers we are working with are reliable. Special attention is paid to the information tracking system that the company has been using.

At some point during this stage there is a sea change in the attitude of the team. It generally comes with the first 'I didn't know that' moment. We begin to discover things about the company - its strengths, weaknesses, opportunities and threats - that were not part of the accepted mythology.

Quite often, we end up doing an assessment of each member of the senior team. We look for imbalances, indications of internal friction or inefficiency, information mismatches, broken decision processes, cul-de-sacs and backwaters and informal relationships that have been negatively affecting results.

The process can take from a couple weeks to a two months. By the time we are finished, we have a clear picture of the context within which the business development function is going to be built.

The next phase of the process begins with a strategic planning retreat. I like to organize these off site. It is important to get the team into a supportive environment and away from the ordinary routine of the office. My favorite venue is a short cruise. Over the years, I have organized many of these retreats and a cruise ship seems to be the best option for a number of reasons. First, it is a convivial venue that takes the team out of their customary patterns. Second, they are a captive audience free of distractions. Third, the cruise lines provide state of the art meeting facilities. Fourth, the cost is roughly sixty percent of a land-based venue. And fifth, there are plenty of opportunities to process the results of our work between sessions.

A typical strategic retreat spans two or three days. The first session is focused on a presentation of my findings and generally takes most of the morning. I systematically lay out those findings and an analysis of them. The result is a holistic picture coupled with a series of recommendations for going forward and a schedule for the balance of the retreat complete with a list of sessions focused on specific issues. This systematic approach provides structure for the process and keeps the team from jumping from issue to issue - a tendency that is both unproductive and inefficient.

The objective of the first session is to get general agreement that the picture presented is accurate and it is followed by a series of meetings which, in planned order, focus on key areas. My preference is to complete that initial session and then allow the group to break for lunch. We don't organize a formal lunch but allow the group to divide up and head out as they see fit. One of the great things about a cruise ship is that there are generally ten to twelve places for these groups to visit. This is critical because it allows individuals and subgroups to process what has been presented.

The second session begins after lunch. Most often it focuses on the present and intended business base of the company. Many of the areas that were thought to be the 'way to go' have been tested by the sharper picture of the company. One CEO observed that "we were thinking that our major push should be into a particular client but now I realize that was not well thought out. We simply don't have the quals to support that effort credibly". The group is tasked to turn assumptions into tested assumptions and to question each one aggressively. Most teams get into this with relish with members take turns playing the devil's advocate. Discussions get very animated and humor mixes in with the seriousness of the task.

I often use newsprint and an easel to record the results of the discussion. Most often we end up with lots of them taped to the walls. Sometimes I call a 'wandering break' that has team members moving from sheet to sheet and adding comments. We then reconvene and re-think. This second session takes most of the afternoon. By the time we break, the team members mind's are full of ideas, new realizations and insights. It's time for a margarita, a trip to the hot tub, a great dinner and maybe a show or visit to the casino.

Dinner is a time when the team comes back together. I enforce a 'no business' rule. *"You can discuss anything you want except business, the day's sessions or tomorrow's work. This is a time to relax and have some fun."* That request works most of the time. Occasionally, I have to crack the whip.

The next day begins as a continuation of the prior session, but, this time, our task is to find a focus for the business development strategy. The team is tasked with finding 'solid ground for expansion' in the near term. It also must build and test a vision for expansion of the company's business base over the next several years. the prior day was focused on investigating alternatives. The second day is for selecting from among them and weaving the selections into a coherent strategy.

Most teams come to terms with the gravity of the undertaking during this session. They realize that what they decide will determine the direction of the company and the focus of the business development efforts. They are now crafting a strategy. If the devil's advocate role dominated the afternoon session of the prior day, it is a collaborative and colligate approach that needs to emerge during this session. Consensus is built and tested, decisions are made, and the outlines of an approach begin to become clear. This is the 'heavy lifting' part of the retreat.

I generally prefer that lunch on the second day finds the team all in the same place. They have worked hard and, with each other's help, made real progress. It is time for a small celebration.

The afternoon session is focused on the implications of the strategy settled on. The question on the table is "OK, we have decided to go in these directions. Now how do we make it work? How do we get there?" Much of this session is focused on the operation and resourcing of the company. By the end of the session we have a holistic plan for the company.

The morning session of the next day is focused on developing metrics. The 'how do we know we are making progress' conversation represents the beginnings of an effort to prepare for implementation. It is serves to assure team-wide buy-in to the plan. Each team members is assigned a set of metrics and commits to meeting or exceeding expectations.

During the afternoon's session, we finally turn to designing the business development part of the team. By now we have a very good picture of the qualities, connections, capabilities and experience that will make for new team members. The discussion revolves around those issues with all team members weighing in. Soon they are able to describe each new team member in great detail. We also focus on the growth of the capability. The team will integrate new hires with branding initiatives, resourcing, performance metrics and the kind of advisory board that is described later in this book.

By the time the strategic planning retreat comes to a close at the closing dinner, we have a clear understanding of the present situation, a detailed road map for a way forward, a resourcing plan, a mutually agreed on set of performance metrics and a team that is determined to execute. The next step is to put all of this before a review panel of highly experienced and well connected experts.

Red-Teaming

Every time I have organized the kind of retreat described above, the team comes back on fire. They are invigorated by the experience and share a common vision and purpose that maybe hasn't been there since the early days. But, I have warned them that we face a major test.

Within a week of returning, they face a red-team that is determined to evaluate and, if necessary, pick apart, their plan. The red-team is made up of very experienced people who know the company and team very well and are committed to helping both succeed. Their role is to make sure that the plan is sound and has a good chance of succeeding.

As you can imagine, there is always a bit of tension in the air the morning of the red-teaming. The performance of management will be tested. They need to communicate and then defend the plan. They know that the charge given the red-team members is 'show no mercy'. This is not the time to let anybody slide by or phone it in. Management know that. The will have to be at the top of their game.

The red-team members have been given the details of the plan with enough information to allow them to do their own diligence. Many of them have current, high-level contacts within the intended customer base. They also have a fairly clear idea of the qualifications, capabilities and potential within the company.

I like to start the red-teaming first thing in the morning. Often it is set for the first Saturday after the planning retreat. It is held off-site in a conference room and generally runs through lunch and well into the afternoon. We take as much time as we need.

The schedule of presentations follows the pattern of the planning retreat. First up is the CEO and a presentation of the overall plan. That is followed by a presentation by the senior business development member of the team. (sometimes that is also the CEO) Third comes the resourcing and reorganization plan which is followed by a presentation of the performance metrics. The fourth presentation focuses on the expansion of the team and a description of the new team members.

My red-teams are very aggressive in testing critical assumptions. One CEO described it as getting "pushed and pulled through a meat grinder".

Once the presentations are finished, the management team leaves the room and the red-team meets in executive session. What follows is a free flowing discussion of the plan and its viability. The nature of the discussion turns from critical analysis to 'how likely is this going to work and how can we contribute to improving the chances of success'. The red-team can deliberate for hours. More than once, they have gone through dinner.

The process comes to a conclusion on Monday morning when selected members of the red-team meet with management. They deliver their assessment of the plan and recommendations for improvement.

Implementation

Management begins to implement the plan by bringing the broader team into the conversation. This involves a series of meetings with groups of employees. The objective is to get everybody on the same page.

The red-team meets with management three weeks after launch of the implementation and every three months thereafter. Progress is measured against the agreed upon performance metrics, the plan is adjusted based on experience and modifications are implemented by management.

Implementation - Getting Started

Let's say that the management's plan has passed muster with the red-team. It has been modified based on inputs from a range of sources and is ready to be shared with the employees. Now things shift from thinking about doing to doing. As one of my early mentors was fond of saying, "*it's not what you say that matters, it's what actually happens*".

Activity needs to begin on multiple fronts. First and foremost, the organization needs to be prepared to receive and culturally integrate the new team members. It is important to keep in mind that you are not expanding the team by bringing on minor variations of your current team - the one that got you to where you are. These will be very different team members and will seem out of pattern to most of that team. You have to be careful and adopt a systematic and professional approach. Do it right, and a new and brighter future will open up.

There are issues that will need attention. Procedures will have to be modified. Reporting and information flow patterns will have to be changed to accommodate the new reality. An example might help.

In the past, the technical line managers might have been the main source of intelligence about new opportunities. The information gathered was passed to someone in the senior team; maybe either the CEO or COO. Perhaps these opportunities were reviewed by an informal executive committee with decisions being based primarily on the likelihood of winning the business and the gross margins that could be achieved. The new organization will require that this pattern be changed. There will now be a senior team member in charge of all business development activities and that person will have a much broader range of issues to keep in focus. The targeting criteria will become much more defined. Targeted new business must fit into the strategic plan. Some business, although obtainable, will be foregone because it doesn't fit.

In the past, it might have been normal for technical line managers to be compensated for gathering and delivering important intelligence. It is important to the process that they remain incentivized. That information must continue to flow. The intelligence that they gather is invaluable to continued success. But now, they will be receiving guidance from the business development team. This guidance will take into consideration such issues as branding, targeting, advantages that the company has in certain areas and the strategic plan that is being implemented. More and more the company will be pursuing new business not so much because it is available but because it fits into the overall plan.

It is also important that the information that flows up from the technical line managers reaches and is taken seriously by the business development team. This intelligence will help them decide what is possible and avoid chasing business which is not winnable.

Another example is the modification of the client relations management process that your company has been using. Once the business development team is in place, there will be more inputs to the system, a need for more precise information, closer coordination and more people accessing and acting on the data. Information will flow upwards to a committee made up of business development, human resources, financial control and operations team members. They will use the data to guide the implementation of the strategic plan. Their decisions will direct business development efforts.

Two areas in particular will change because of this. Human resources will have to coordinate more closely with business development. New business won will mean a need to expand the number of employees and that must be done in a systematic and coordinated way. Human resources must deliver before the business arrives. Delays will mean problems in capturing and delivering on the contracts. Finance and financial control will also have to up their game. First, they will have to arrange for the financial resources needed to capture and deliver on the new business - including forward funding of the expansion of the employee base. Second, they will have to put the necessary reporting procedures in place well in advance.

The strategic plan and expansion of the senior team will mean a change in the roles of team members. Some areas that either the CEO or COO have historically covered will now be the responsibility of the business development team. New bases will have to be covered as the systems grow in both size and complexity. Other areas that were covered by the CEO or COO will have to be delegated. Reporting patterns, spans of control and responsibilities will alter to meet the needs of an expanded organization.

The message here is that real change requires real change in your organization, management and oversight of the operations of the company.

Implementation - Recruiting

Senior management needs to begin to organize and then kick off the recruiting process. If you remember my comments earlier on, it will not surprise you that I prefer an alternative to the standard approach of gathering resumes and arranging interviews. There is a better way.

The first step is to have the process managed independently. I have done this on many occasions and can tell you that it really does work better. The second step is to involve the wide range of search contacts; extending well beyond those of the management team.

Part of the reason that this is such a good idea goes to the nature of the people being interviewed. Business development types are very good at managing first impressions and targeting and achieving personal objectives. It is one of the characteristics that make them good at what they do. When I am involved in such a process, I insist on taking the first interviews without the participation of any member of the management team. This allows for the evaluation of candidates while avoiding the 'love at first sight' syndrome that can carry great risk. Once candidates have passed the first hurdle, they are introduced to management with a set of recommendations, an assessment of their strengths and weaknesses and a judgment as to how well they might fit both into the current management team and the overall strategic plan.

Another reason why this approach works so well is that the pressure being felt by management is not a factor in the initial interviews. Senior members of management tend to want to find a solution and move on. Although this is an important part of the later process, it can result in precipitous decisions during early interviews.

A third reason why this approach works better has to do with the range of experience and contacts of the person managing the initial process. Over the years I have developed working relationships with a wide range of head hunters. They are not all even remotely the same either in their abilities to deliver talent or to understand exactly what you are looking for in a new hire. But, with experience and guidance, they become much better at understanding the needs and working to meet them. There is no substitute for extended experience. As a result, I have a series of relationships with head hunters who know how I operate. That is a major advantage.

Finally, the process allows the candidates to learn about the company and its potential from a source that they will more easily trust. The 'give and take' negotiations that will follow do not interfere with this. By the time that management meets with candidates, they have a clear idea of the opportunity.

Once a cadre of candidates has been identified, the process of interviewing goes much the same as you might expect. Management reviews each resume and initial interviews are organized with candidates that they want to pursue. I operate as an 'honest broker' and make sure that important questions are well addressed and that negotiations proceed towards the most favorable results for all involved.

One key to making the process work better is to focus forward during the interviews. You will ask the general questions at first but need to get to specifics rather quickly. Both you and the candidate should be discussing what will happen if they join the team. Their responses should be detailed and focused appropriately. Candidates that have not taken the time to figure out where your company is going will probably not do that after they are on the team. A prudent interview process results in a six to twelve month plan for the new team member; a plan which has been carefully matched against your strategic plan. If you end up with less than this you are rolling the dice. That is gambling not business.

One of the benefits of a good interview process is that the candidates come in contact with a wild range of team members. That will allow the normal 'attitude checks' and help you decide if the person is going to fit in personally as well as professionally. This is an important part of the process. Remember that the personality makeup of the business development types is going to be substantially different from that of most of your team. A wide range of meetings in different settings is a good way to see if the sensitivity to those differences is there on both sides.

There are some imaginative ways to manage this part of the process. One that I particularly liked was suggested by a very creative CEO. She was managing the hiring process and decided to involve one of the candidates in an upcoming educational program that the company was offering to its clients. The nature of the program required members of the team to cooperate closely. The time pressures put them into ASAP mode. It was something of a pressure cooker. The challenge was to manage the pressure in a way that it did not interfere with the advance towards the objective. There were plenty of opportunities for clashed of egos. But the candidate came through with flying colors and the program was a complete success.

Implementation - Cultural Integration

One of the greatest risks that building a business development team brings is the possibility that the team assembled will become a 'side show'; a group apart from the balance of the management team. In the field of mergers and acquisitions, roughly seventy percent of all acquisitions are either dilutive or neutral when it comes to shareholder value. It is widely agreed that most of the problems occur because of a failure to integrate the cultures of the two companies. It is worth taking that lesson when considering the challenges of standing up a business development team. Think of building a new business development team as an acquisition of a culturally distinct company.

The culture of most good business development teams is heavily focused on hunting and capturing. Most effective corporate teams are closer to farmers than hunters. In some ways, the cultural integration challenge is much like that of mixing oil and water. Anybody who has tried that realizes that you can shake things up pretty well and get what's called an emulsion. But, if you let the mixture set quietly, you quickly end up with one floating on top of the other. That is the way it tends to be with business development and operations. It is hard to overstate the difficulties of this cultural integration. It is one of the most difficult challenges that any CEO faces.

The tensions between the two 'world views' is such that, left alone, they will inevitably separate into cliques. If they do, much of the investment that has been made will be wasted.

I have worked with companies where the separation was complete. The business development types didn't talk to the operating side of the company. One result was that they kept pursuing and capturing business that was not in the best interest of the company. In one extreme case, the business development team brought in an equipment resale contract. The company was in the software development business! In another case, the COO gave the business development presentation during an all-hands retreat; with the business development team lamely looking on.

The responsibility to maintain the intermixing rests with the senior management team. Close coordination among them (including the senior business development officer) is essential. But coordination needs to extend well beyond that. The two cultures need to be intertwined all the way down to the client interface.

There is a particular challenge at the client interface that needs special attention. Prior to standing up the business development team, clients probably saw the technical line managers as the primary point of contact when it came to new business. The situation may remain mostly the same but, if the process is running correctly, the line managers will be more directed; focused on the direction that the new business search will take. That means that they will have to have the information and guidance to correctly represent the newer, more focused interests of the company. It also means that there will be circumstances when it is a good idea to bring along one of the business development team members. The protocols have to be worked out ahead of time. You don't want them making it up as they go along.

It is important to realize that, when well structured, business development interpenetrates your entire organization. Everybody should be informed, alert and aware of their responsibilities to contribute.

Implementation - Metrics

A critical part of launching a business development team is the agreement on the performance metrics reached during the interviewing process. Candidates should know what the strategic plan is, how it will be tactically deployed, their role in implementation and the way that their performance will be measured. One of the most expensive mistakes that management teams make is to skip over this process altogether or simply brush over it by hitting the 'high points'. The key to a quick and effective start is a solid agreement on performance metrics. It is very important that the senior management team buy into this dynamic and insist on implementation after hiring. Perhaps a 'war story' will illustrate what I mean.

I once built a team for an owner/CEO. During the interview process I had each candidate draw up a business development plan - a road map for their first year on the team. Because this new hire constituted a major expansion of the team, I was persistent and insistent that the plan be well developed and vetted. I also required that the candidate 'own' the plan and agree that implementation was a 'first priority' if they were brought onto the team.

I studied the offered plans carefully. We ended up with two candidates for the lead role. Both had developed, submitted and defended fairly detailed plans. The choice between the two was up to the owner of the business. He made his choice, an offer was made and accepted and then the wheels began to fall off.

I was appalled by what I found during the first performance review meeting. The owner had 'taken the guy under his wing' and treated him more like a colleague than a team member responsible for identifying, pursuing and capturing business. Their conversations seemed to center around a series of increasingly complex spread sheets which they were incessantly manipulating. The original plan had been tossed aside.

The new team member seemed more a member of a country club than a professional member of the team. When I asked about the strategic plan, he 'blew up' and the owner defended him. The result was that there was no strategic plan for building the business. You can imagine how it went from there. Within six months the new guy was fired and the owner ended up merging the company with another small operation.

Metrics matter and preparation must have implications beyond the vetting process. Business development types are hunters and need to be strongly tasked for performance. The good ones expect it. Metrics are the mechanism for achieving that.

One of the principal benefits of establishing and enforcing metrics it that it will help manage conflicts later on. If all parties sign on to carefully crafted metrics, then discussions will be forced to that of implementation and performance under the metrics. More than once, such metrics have helped me put a stop to mudslinging outbreaks.

Implementation - Pipelines

One of the great games that business development types play centers around the pipeline; the volume of business identified and in the process of being pursued or captured. It is a matter of pride for them to have a big pipeline. The 'mine's bigger than yours' syndrome is so ubiquitous that most of them fall into it without thinking. Management teams can get sucked into this game and become impressed by the large and growing numbers.

The trap in pipelines is in taking the numbers seriously without testing their validity or value. There is all sorts of software available to manage a pipeline and most of it obscures fundamental weaknesses in the business development strategy. Cascading numbers can hide flaws in the approach. Graphs and spreadsheets can obfuscate rather than clarify.

I worked with one company that had a very substantial run rate and pipeline. The business development team was proud of that pipeline. But, when we took a closer look at it, we found that half the business in the pipeline was 'under water'; it was going to cost the company money just to deliver on the contracts. The company had been so busy pursuing business that it did not check to see if it was profitable business.

Another company with a growing pipeline found that the business development efforts were so unfocused that the pipeline was littered with opportunities that lay outside of the company's core quals. When we analyzed the implications we found that the unique characteristic of much of it, when combined with the need to bring in 'contract expertise' to supplement the team, was going make the business unprofitable.

I remember one particular company with an impressive pipeline. The Chairman of the Board had asked me to 'take a look'. One of my first steps was to sit in on the weekly business development review sessions. About the third session I realized that I was hearing a lot of what had been said in prior meetings. I asked a simple question, "*What is the velocity of each piece of business through the pipeline*?" After getting a few mystified looks, I repeated the question. Again blank stares. Finally I said, "*how much of this business is in exactly the same state of development as it was three months ago*?" After all the hemming and hawing was over, the answer was about two-thirds. That meant that two-thirds of the business in the pipeline was not moving towards capture.

There was an interesting development as a result of the conversation described above. Once we began cutting out those targets that were not moving and, in the judgment of the business development team, were not likely to move towards capture, the result was a greatly slimmed down pipeline; less than half of the original number. But now, with fewer unproductive distractions, the business development team went to work moving the remaining targets along. The result was that the company had a significant increase in its run rate and a much more productive business development process. Sometimes less really is more.

A key characteristic of a good pipeline is the velocity of targets. A second key is the coherence of the targets and the close match with the strategic plan.

Implementation - Monitoring

The real challenges of managing a business development team begin once it has been established. To return to an earlier metaphor, the farmers are busy doing the business of the company and managing its operations. The business development team members gather their weapons and sortie each day in search of game. The hunters are a strange lot in the eyes of the farmers. But the farmers need to find a way to constructively manage and direct the hunters. Hunting brings short-term success; farming builds long-term value. Both have to work together if the company is going to grow.

The first, and most important, link between the two camps is the relationship between the CEO and the senior business development team member. This needs to be an open, no-BS and professional relationship. Both need to be committed to a collaboration which bridges the chasm that separates the two cultures. In fact, in the best of all worlds, the CEO has a foot in both camps and, when required, acts as the senior business development officer for the company.

The two, in partnership, need to tend the relationships between the two camps. And that tending needs to involve the entire company. Both need to be constantly looking for indications of schisms forming or tensions developing. Actions need to be coordinated and effective when such risks appear. "An ounce of prevention is worth a pound of cure", is a good guiding principle.

One of the most effective ways to keep communications flowing is to arrange regular contact between the two camps. I like to extend this well beyond the work environment. One of the most effective ways was discovered during an all-hands retreat. An Example might help here.

I was working with a company that had just stood up a business development team. The company had an all hands retreat schedule and we took advantage of that opportunity to deepen the relationships between the two camps. The retreat was multi-day and offsite.

During the first day, we had a full day of work; seminars, speakers and breakout working groups. We made sure that the two camps were intermixed during each session and took pains to make sure they did not sit apart from each other. The next day was for play. We organized a series of games and other events. The standing rule was no 'clique' teams. The two camps had to join, collaborate and cooperate in order to win.

What was amazing was that characteristics related to hunters or farmers were valuable in some games while not in others. Also, some valuable characteristics were not related at all. For example, in the volleyball tournament, tall and athletic was good. There were tall hunters and farmers. When it came to the trivia game, quick thinking and a good memory were important. Farmers tended to be better at trivia. When it came to the scavenger hunt, ... Well, I think you get the drift.

By the end of the retreat we could see those cross cultural relationships blossoming. The CEO told me afterwards that that alone was worth the cost of the retreat.

The lesson is that it takes persistence, focus and creativity to get the two camps to work together. The measure of management is how well it meets and masters this challenge.

Managing Conflict

As sure as the sun will rise tomorrow, there is going to be conflicts between the business development team and the rest of your organization. As an old mentor used to say, *'count on it, accept in, deal with it and get on with it."* If you think your company is going to inhabit a quiet meadow where the sun always shines, the rain is warm and comforting and the flowers always bloom on time, you are in for a rude shock. Moving out of the 'village stage' means moving onto the 'fast lane' and that is more like bumper cars than shading under a spreading elm.

You will be amazed at the range of conflicts that arise. They will come at you from all sides and require a steady hand, an allegiance to agreements and metrics and patience - lots of patience. Here are a few examples from my experiences with a range of companies:

o   A fire fight broke out because human resources had not populated the 'beach' with the right kinds of new hires. They failed to match the needs with their recruiting results.

o   Another broke out because the chief financial officer had failed to get the required accounting and financial control systems in place. As this was a requirement prior to funds transfer, it put the new piece of business at risk.

o   A business development team had pursued and won a piece of business that was outside the quals of the company. The got so enamored of the size of the contract that they overstepped the strategic plan.

o   A COO made an arbitrary decision to transfer some of the people and resources to a specific contract just as business development was bringing in a big piece of new business. Both human resources and finance were affected.

o   The business development team issued guidance to the technical line managers that wasn't clear. As a result they shifted their focus and began to give conflicting signals to their customer base about new business objectives.

o   The CEO, during a meeting with a number of clients of the company, made representations and commitments that were at variance with both the strategic plan and the quals of the company. Resetting expectations set the business development process back and cost the company momentum.

Maybe you get the idea. Mixing oil and water is never forever and, when the two cultures begin to pull apart, these and many other tensions can arise. So what is the best way to keep the fires from flaring up?

o   Remember the old saying, "an idle mind is the devil's workshop"? The first prophylactic strategy is to keep up the pace and everybody focused on the road ahead. It is easier to brush off flare-ups when you are busy pushing one foot forcefully ahead of the other.

o   Pick up the vibes early and deal with them. You need a very sensitive set of antennae to do that but a 'stitch in time does save nine'. One of your best sources of advanced intelligence will be the executive assistants and secretaries. Keep your finger lightly on the web strands and move quickly when a tremor occurs.

o   Celebrate the 'heading off of conflict'. This is one strategy that is easily overlooked but is very potent when it comes to developing a culture that naturally anticipated and avoids conflict. Remember, avoiding a situation that could have cost the company resources, team members and reputation is a good reason to celebrate.

o   Revisit the plan and metrics regularly. If you reinforce the common understanding and agreements surrounding the plan and metrics, you will reduce the probabilities of flare-ups.

o   Pay attention to the levels of enthusiasm and confidence within your broader team. Happy campers are less likely to harbor the kinds of resentment that can explode into conflict.

o   Make allowances for your people being human. Remember, everybody has bad days and deserves to be treated with consideration when they do. You should help your team understand that as well. The more humanly they treat each other, the easier it will be for them to deal with tensions and resolve conflicts.

In Summary

Every growing company faces the challenges outlined above. It is unavoidable. Success brings them on and success is a good thing. The real measure is how well management meets and masters these challenges.

Every company goes through a relatively predictable set of stages. In what I call the 'village stage', your own contacts and instincts are able to meet the challenges of building a company. But sooner or later, and sooner the more successful you are, it becomes necessary to cast off the 'village stage' and move on to a more professional approach to managing and growing the company. As much as you may want to remain within the relatively comfortable context, you must lead your team into the new and unfamiliar.

Building a well-integrated and functional business development part of your team will be one of the most difficult of these challenges. Little of what you have used to get your company off the ground and to profitability will help you. You will need to develop new skills and adopt new approaches to meet and master the challenge.

It is important to remember that where you are going constitutes a new phase in your company's development. By bringing a new type of team member onboard, you are introducing dynamics into the mix that can radically destabilize the company's culture. It is necessary to do this. But it is also necessary to do it with care and forethought. Further growth is essential if the company is going to thrive but such steps bring risks that will test your abilities and those of your team. You can do it if you do it well.

Advisory Boards As Business Development Engines

The first section of this book focused on building and managing a business development team. In the following section, I want to introduce a potent approach to making business development live up to its name.

What follows assumes that your company has meet and mastered the challenges of establishing and managing an effective business development team.

The core idea in the following chapters is that an advisory board, appropriately structured, tasked and managed is, by far, the most effective way to magnify the potential of a business development team and drive the run rate of a company.

The design for the boards comes out of years of experience in building and managing them. During those years, I have discovered how subtle and demanding the process of standing up a board can be. Getting four to six very well connected and highly experienced individuals to become forceful advocates is a real challenge. But, if successfully done, the results can be truly amazing.

The early chapters in this section deal with some of the problems I have encountered with advisory boards. I then describe the process of designing, populating and managing a board focused solely on increasing revenues.

Advisory Boards That Don't Produce

I build and manage advisory boards as business development engines for emerging and well-established companies. Properly designed and managed, they are the single most powerful component of business development that I have ever found – bar none! The process of setting up and managing the boards is one of the most fulfilling roles that I play.

I am often contacted by CEOs who have become frustrated with the lack of effectiveness of their business development strategies and have decided to seek out another way. They might have read one of my articles on advisory boards and contacted me to see if my approach could make a difference with their company. Others are referred by friends. Either way, it is the first step in a journey that changes forever the way the CEO looks at the process of business development and their role in it.

Many of these companies already have advisory boards that haven't been very productive. Dissatisfaction with the lack of results is often a primary driver. Mostly CEOs are frustrated by unfulfilled promises and are determined to find a better way. These conversations, and the engagements that have followed, have yielded a pile of war stories. Patterns have emerged. Here are seven of the most common reasons that advisory boards fail to produce significant value:

The Logical Imperative

Advisory boards get formed for all sorts of reasons - most of them ineffectual and some flatly unwise. In most cases boards seemed to have been formed under what I call the 'logical imperative'.

"Of course we'll have an advisory board! Let's pull one together just like those guys did. Of course it will focus on advising us on technology issues – or management issues. It will be a coffee clutch – a collegiate meeting of like minds. We'll meet once a month – or (somewhat later) once a quarter. It will be great!"

Well, maybe you get the picture. But it isn't great and such boards do not produce results. The point is that the founders have not carefully thought through why they are forming the board. For the most part they have not even thought through a proper mission. Most have no real experience with a highly productive board and end up doing what seems like the logical thing to do at the time. The process seems so intuitive that the board seems to form itself. Many times it is a 'peer-gathering' - *"I'll be on your board and you on mine."* These boards are almost always net-zero undertakings at best and net-negative in the long run. Logical imperatives tend to lead to ineffectual gaggles rather than productive, working boards.

Dangerous Liaisons

For some reason some CEOs never seem to put the words 'corporate' and 'espionage' together. They build advisory boards (I suspect out of a suspicion of personal or professional inadequacy) to advise them on technology and/or management issues. Over and over I come across boards that regularly see the latest and neatest advances of a company; boards that are populated with people who have interests outside their board participation. *"Oh, no – I trust these people,"* I am often told. Such statements remind me of a story about a young woman who was visiting her spinster aunt. While they were having tea in the parlor a cat wandered in with a litter of new kittens.

"Oh, aren't they so cute," said the visitor.

"Yes they are – but I can't figure out how they happened. Fluffy is a house cat and she never goes outside."

As she was talking a clearly virile tom cat came into the room and stretched sensuously. *"What about him,"* inquired the girl?*"*

"Oh no, couldn't be Tom," said the aunt. *"He's her brother!"*

I leave you to follow the story to where it leads – but the point should be clear enough. Too late smart is, first and foremost, too late.

Who's Minding the Store?

Often when reviewing the history and mission of ineffectual boards I find that there is no clear mission for the board, no defined strategy for managing the board and no formal metrics for measuring its effectiveness and performance. The CEO is nominally in charge but the board is managed only during the times just preceding, during and immediately following its meetings. For the rest of the time it is mostly ignored with little contact between board members and the senior team.

Additionally, the lack of clear, effective and enforced metrics has defined a culture that virtually guarantees little or no production. Many times board members serve based on a 'verbal agreement' – and as Sam Goldwyn used to say *"a verbal agreement isn't worth the paper it's written on!"*

When it comes to such a board, members see leadership without purposefulness and participation without responsibility. Meetings tend to be rambling discussions on management style, Monday morning quarterbacking the CEO and water cooler type hashing and re-hashing of corporate gossip. Board members, who see a leadership without apparent purpose or concern with performance metrics, react similarly. These boards tend to discuss the same issues over and over again until the members get bored and the merry-go-round slows down and finally stops.

What Mission Statement?

"What's it good for? Absolutely nothing!" Logical imperatives, dangerous liaisons and inattentive management lead to wasted energy, lost opportunities and negative branding. Yes, negative branding! I have dismantled boards and interviewed lots of 'advisors' – some of whom have spent many frustrating years on ineffectual boards. Often I was sure that the ears of the senior corporate team had to be burning. And these are supposed to be their friends!

Oh, you think that your advisors always say such good things about you? Well, wake up and smell the decaying flesh! If you are wasting their time and the company's resources, if you are risking their reputation, if you are acting more like a den mother than a CEO, if your ego seems to be the most important part of your anatomy, what do you think they are going to say?

A board should, from its very conception, have a clear mission statement. Board members should be recruited with that mission statement front-and-center. They should clearly understand what will be expected of them, how they will be paid and what will happen if expectations are not met. Without this, forget the idea of having a board. It will just become a kamikaze raid on a vacant lot!

Wisdom on the Cheap

There are CEOs and senior team members who are penny wise and pound foolish. Visit any chat room dedicated to start-ups and you can listen in on the same conversation over and over. Most of them start with the premise that it is unwise to pay advisors in any but an incentivized way – in other words only based on the results they generate. Although incentivized compensation is an important component of any good advisory agreement, there needs to be a base of recognition for service. But these cynics take the argument to the extreme. In one recent thread a series of so-called CEOs weighed in with almost identical observations. Most of them had war stories about consultants that had taken their money and produced very little. As the single-perspective discussion reached its peak, I introduced two ideas into the mix. First, aren't selections of non-productive consultants a direct reflection on the 'decider' and the inadequacies of the process of selection and engagement? And second, if you limit the pool of possible consultants to those who will work only for incentivized compensation, don't you filter out professionals whose track record of production puts them in a position to require non-incentivized compensation? You would think that I had dropped a cat into a box full of mice! *"Oh no, it wasn't me ... it was 'them'."* The so-called CEOs all considered it a failure on the part of the consultant. 'Blame the other' was the theme!

Psychologists have a term for this kind of denial of responsibility. Look, you either believe that there are people out there who have knowledge and connections that can help you or you don't. If you do, you go out and find them then make agreements which reflect the reality of the market for their services. The onus is on you to search effectively and reach productive agreements; even if it taxes your company's resources.

Any expenditure must yield a return on investment and any agreement must specify performance metrics. No professional would find that onerous. My experience is that

70

no well connected person with a serious intent and ability to make a contribution will give away that potential in exchange for a purely conditional compensation. In other words, you get what you pay for! CEOs who can successfully navigate these waters have a substantial leg up on their competitors. It is a skill that needs to be learned both to avoid the waste of non-productive relationships and to reap the benefits of productive ones. Wisdom on the cheap is just another tilt at yet another windmill.

Making Love to the Inertia

Many of my engagements begin with a dismantling of an existing advisory board. Most of these boards were formed amid much enthusiasm; with members happy to have a chance to contribute. But over time, and with a declining enthusiasm, they have simply ceased to function. For the most part little of this is the fault of the board members. They are, after all, not officers of the company and have been asked to help it succeed by people who they expected to help them do just that. But inertia is overwhelming in the face of the lack of intent and intent is driven by leadership. Management often falls in love with the inertia that these boards allow and that is a recipe for disaster.

My suspicion is that, in the face of a wildly chaotic world, they see the board as a kind of oasis; a quiet place to go to have peaceful conversations with fellow travelers. Without connection to the imperatives that are driving the rest of the company, these boards languish into unproductively neutral cultures. Finally they ossify into a mass of inertia. The end has arrived. It doesn't matter how much longer the board is in existence. It becomes the proverbial 'dead man walking'. Execution is often the merciful thing.

We're Ready for Prime Time - Not

I get this one a lot! A CEO reads some of my articles and comes to the conclusion that *"I've just got to have one of those boards."* So we have our initial meeting. I talk a lot about how the company has to ready itself for a board. The middle-level business development types will become a liability and need to be replaced with far more experienced team members. The resourcing of targeting, proposal development, red-team and capture have to be beefed up if the company is going to take advantage of the opportunities that an advisory board can make available. There is a lot to be done in getting ready.

I emphasize that this is a complex process that has to be approached professionally and with careful preparation. Then it comes. *"I don't think that we need all this 'getting ready'. Why don't you just go out and get me some advisors?"* At first I am patient and explain that very important people will not be willing to risk their reputations with a company ill prepared to take advantage of their assistance. Then I get something like:

> *"This is obvious and it should be a concern of yours. However, not in our case. We do have considerable experience working with 'very senior and highly professional' people and also, we are quite capable of executing."*

This is a direct quote from one CEO whose advisory board had been completely unproductive and whose company was about to run out of resources because of management's complete failure to generate significant volumes of new business! The hard truth is that the advisors that I place on a board care deeply about preserving and extending their reputations. They are not about to risk them on such representations. They know a whole lot better than that! You should as well. This mutual understanding is the gateway to a more productive way of relating to the process of business development for your company.

They Can Work – and Work Beyond Your Wildest Dreams

The single most amazing thing about these discussions is that, despite all of the hazards and misunderstandings, many of them lead to productive engagements that produce results. Perhaps one out of three CEOs gets through the kinds of challenges outlined above. And, out of those, somewhere around four in ten actually engage me to begin the process of forming a board.

In an important way the process is self-selecting. CEOs who can understand and adapt to a new approach to business development are precisely the right candidates for having, and learning to benefit from, an advisory board. It is these four-in-thirty that make the entire process such a joy for me and the professionals associated with me. For, once the preliminaries are out of the way, the real magic begins. The old saw is that 'nothing succeeds like success.' Well nothing feels better than helping someone succeed beyond their wildest dreams.

Dysfunctional Advisory Boards – A Family of Problems

A well designed, populated and managed advisory board can bring substantial benefits. This is particularly true when it comes to the process of business development. Such a board can help senior management succeed beyond their wildest dreams. But there are reefs and shoals that need to be avoided.

Often a new client will have an existing advisory board. One of my early tasks in such situations is to '*fix it*'. At least that's how the CEO tends to put it. Most of these boards have common characteristics and most are indicators that the board needs to be dismantled and replaced.

The primary negative indicator is almost always a lack of productivity. Many have been in existence for years but have yet to directly make significant contributions. A secondary indicator is unproductive board meetings, which may have started out monthly but now occur less and less frequently. Members have either lost enthusiasm or patience and become observers rather than players. Meetings tend to occur, if at all, without much prior preparation and with little, if any, structured agenda. The culture seems to be focused on maintaining camaraderie rather than high value creation. As a friend of mine used to say "*the wrong is over but the malady lingers on.*"

Some boards have become completely virtual. These represent a major effort in duel negative branding by senior management. They are indicative both of a failure of management and of a corporate culture of waste and inattention. Board members tend to fall into the 'rent-a-name' category. Not only do these boards typically have to be dismantled but a campaign often needs to be mounted to overcome the accumulated damage to the corporate image. This is particularly true within its client base. Doing it poorly is often worse than not doing it at all.

Many of these boards include members who have been serving for years. Little if any tracking of their contributions to the company's growth has been done. In fact, there is often a total lack of metrics which define effective board service.

The development of appropriate advisory board metrics is elementary school math. So the real question is, *"why do many companies with advisory boards not have appropriate metrics in place?"* I would suggest that the answer lies in a) how un-seriously management takes the existence, value and potential contributions of the board and b) how poorly they take advantage of the opportunities it could create. Of course, such a board will probably, if pressed, prove incapable of delivering solid value anyway.

At a strategic level, the purpose and charge of the board tends to be very poorly drawn. There is often no coherent document which describes either the function of the board or the manner in which its performance and the performance of its members will be measured. Matriculation to board membership tends to be casual. Given this, how effective would you suppose a board will be? How can everybody be on the same page when there is no page?

I see only one appropriate mission for an advisory board and that is driving the company's revenue. A board should be populated by individuals who can help management identify, pursue and capture large pieces of business that management would not be able to without the board's assistance. As a result, board membership should be predicated on the ability of each board member to contribute significantly to the company's growth. Individuals need to be able to open doors, influence decision-makers, advocate for the company and help management organize a highly professional approach to capturing significant new business.

Once this focus is accepted, the evolution of metrics for effective board membership and advisory board performance becomes easy. Additionally the relationship between the board and management, particularly the relationship between the board and the CEO, becomes easier to define.

The compensation scheme for advisory board members is easy to draw. First there should be an annual retainer; a modest sum in recognition of board service. Second there should be a small honorarium for meeting participation and a provision for covering expenses. Most importantly, there should be an incentivized compensation agreement which is calculated based on the volume of business brought in. Finally there should be a provision for achieving equity ownership after certain conditions, particularly conditions that relate to performance, have been met.

There is one characteristic of highly productive advisory boards that I've noticed over the years. And this one is going to stick in the craw of the CEOs who see themselves as chief of everything. The best advisory boards are built by people from outside of the company for the company. They are built by people who specialize in board design, population and management. Home grown boards tend to be underachievers. I think this is the case for two basic reasons. First, CEOs tends to prefer known people that they are comfortable with. These relationships actually limit the board's productivity. Second, the CEO's connections tend to be at levels lower than is needed to populate an effective board.

The first of these can lead to boards that have collegiate but unproductive meetings. They tend towards feel-good societies which massage management's combined egos at the expense of shareholder value. Every board that I have built generates, particularly in its initial meetings, a strong sense of vertigo among senior management. Individual board members, often towards the end of long and highly successful careers, challenge management to get their collective acts together and the company in shape to deal with the increased business that the board can produce.

The second tendency can be more lethal than the first. Board members need to be very senior individuals with a wide range of contacts, current credibility in critical areas and a willingness to actually work through the entire process of identifying, chasing and capturing new business. They need to operate as active and aggressive advocates for the company. Individual board members, who do not meet these basic criteria, will prove unproductive and sometimes destructive, of board operations. 'Rent-a-Name' boards are pure overhead. It is advocacy not introductions that is needed. Board members need to be working partners rather than patrician purveyors of holy water. Members who meet these criteria are extremely hard to find. A critical characteristic of the individual who builds a board is that they have a very wide range of senior contacts and can manage a widely ranging search for effective members.

The design, population and management of an advisory board is one of the most subtle and complex journeys that a company will undertake. Done right, the process can lead to unexpectedly high growth rates. Done poorly, it is a waste of resources and senior management time.

Advisory Boards as Business Development Engines – The Beginnings

A well-constructed and professionally managed advisory board can bring amazing benefits to a company. A poorly designed and managed one is usually a colossal waste of resources. The difference often lays not so much in the idea of an advisory board, but in the execution of that idea by the senior management team, and particularly the CEO. In many cases, the productivity of a company's advisory board is an indication of the effectiveness and sharpness of focus of the senior management team.

In order to show you how it can work, I want to describe the very first advisory board that I built specifically as a business development engine.

My fourth company taught me how to leverage the needs of a client base and fund the launch using customers' money. Beyond a validation of my suspicion that

o   a promising solution to a major problem would draw investment from those who will most benefit (the customers) and

o   involving potential clients intimately in the process of developing solutions to their challenges would ensure their support of the company which then offered those solutions,

Another important lesson was learned; this time quite by accident. This was the company that showed me how an advisory board, if appropriately structured, populated and managed, could radically improve performance.

We had taken up the challenge to revolutionize the way feature films were financed in the US. Once our solution was perfected and business model was in place, we set about managing three flows. The first was the flow of product, in this case film projects that we could finance. The second was the flow of investment dollars which would ensure that we could meet our obligations under the financing agreements. The third was the flow of bank funds to finance the balance of the production budgets.

Informally at first, but more formally later, we formed two working groups that eventually merged into one advisory board. The first group was representatives from the film industry and their bankers. Its task was to organize the flow of investment ready opportunities. The second group was senior representatives of the Wall Street investment banking houses and large accounting firms. Their task was to organize the flow of investment dollars. Initially we spent time working to balance the flows but I soon realized that, if we brought both groups together, we could more closely coordinate the process. Thus the advisory board as a business development engine was born.

What was neat about this approach was that multi-million dollar transactions were often proposed, negotiated and funded during a single advisory board meeting. The process wasn't entirely on automatic pilot but it sure was a lot easier to manage. My team provided the meeting coordination, processing and the post-closing management. We also acted as the coordinator of the overall process and made sure that each interest within the merged groups was fairly served. In the end everybody had a big win and everybody had a respected role in the process.

On reflection, there were at least three major characteristics of this advisory board that were important to its success. The first was that the board had a very well defined and obviously important function to serve. (And I am not referring to driving the run rate of a startup company) When the members came to the meetings there was an anticipation of 'doing business' and 'getting things done'. As a result meeting preparation was very through, materials were provided well in advance and meeting participation was very active.

A second characteristic was that all board members had specific economic interests that the group would help advance. All of the players came to do business and trusted the others (including members of my team) to come to the table in the same spirit. A culture of cooperation emerged and always focused on a common set of goals and understandings that served the individual goals of each participant.

Finally, all discussions were conducted in a spirit of camaraderie and common purpose. Complex settlements would be explored and reached at the table and not left to extended phone discussions that typically involved lawyers and accountants. In other words, the decision makers made the decisions (and compromises) together.

From my team's perspective, the advisory board made life much easier. The flow of product, investment funds and bank loans was organized within one venue. The regular meetings of the board provided a continuity of process that helped to organize a complex situation. Because the 'market' had become so well organized and the 'players' were all recognized as 'friends', the process of arranging and closing financing became 'rationalized'. Much of the uncertainty had been removed. My team got the credit for doing that and the company was seen as a necessary part of the process.

Advisory Boards – Ancillary Benefits

Most CEOs have had experiences with building and managing advisory boards; many have had one or more at their disposal. But much of that experience has been negative or neutral. In many cases, advisory boards tended to be mostly window dressing. In this chapter I would like to focus on some of the ancillary benefits that these boards can bring. In what follows, I will be talking about advisory boards as I build them and not as they exist in their various and less effective forms.

In addition to driving revenue, my advisory boards represent a deep pool of experience in growing and managing businesses. Individuals who should appropriately be placed on such boards for their abilities to help management win more business also tend to have a history of successfully building and managing large companies or organizations. Some of this experience may be in the commercial space while others might have come from the military or senior government service. But the experience is relevant either way. So the first benefit that an advisory board brings, long before it ever targets its first piece of business, is the development of a series of mentoring relationships. As the board begins to settle in, these relationships will begin to deepen. The principal beneficiary of this process is the CEO but other senior members of the team (particularly the head of business development) will also gain support and access to pools of wisdom and experience that it would be difficult for the company to buy outright.

Mentoring relationships are hard to form in this post-modern era. Many CEOs that I come in contact with have never developed a single one; although all of them have expressed a desire to have mentors. An advisory board offers the opportunity for mentoring relationships to develop. A board represents a group of senior executives who are willing to share their experience, judgments and recommendations. This kind of mentoring can be particularly valuable to a CEO who is trying to grow his business but may not have the decades of experience that will be found on the board. It has been my experience that each senior team member finds benefits in these mentoring relationships. In addition to the CEO, the head of business development receives invaluable advice; advice which would cost the company tens if not hundreds of thousands of dollars if they bought it outright.

Learning How To Win

During the first meetings, board members tend to be focused on the management team and the company's organization and resourcing. (Remember that they have decided to put their reputations on the line for the company) Their first order of business is to make sure that their reputation will be enhanced rather than degraded through association with the company. They will want to make sure that the company they have affiliated with, and risked their reputations on, takes the necessary steps both in organization and resourcing that will allow it to take advantage of the opportunities which board members can make available.

The initial series of meetings invariably focuses on these issues of resourcing and organization. Management is pressed to adopt best practices in corporate governance and resourcing. Over time, there tends to be a reduction of expenditures in the purely business development area and an increased emphasis on proposal development, capture team resourcing and management and red teaming. There also tends to be an improved focus in the area of marketing and the targeting of new areas for business development. The board helps management focus on the tactical problems of generating revenue. I have watched as management teams, that were addicted to high-level discussions about markets and strategy, were taken out behind the proverbial woodshed. One of the greatest gifts that an advisory board can give a CEO is to teach them that business is about doing business not talking about doing business.

As a result of working with the board, the management team develops a sharper understanding of what it takes to win, of what is truly excellent and what is merely good. The team raises their standards and takes a giant step in the direction of becoming a truly professional team.

Playing With the Pros

Another ancillary benefit is that, through the advisory board, management is brought into direct contact with senior decision makers and gate keepers. Board members tutor the team on how to approach these senior decision makers. They help them 'up their game' to meet much more stringent standards. Often these lessons are forcefully delivered. Advisers can be quite direct in outlining their expectations. They will insist that the company meet the standards and deliver on time and above requirements. They show team members how to be professionals. I once sat in on a session that a board member had with a Senior Vice President of Business Development. The lesson could be described as 'How to talk to an Admiral'. Although it had to be repeated several time, eventually the SVP mastered the technique.

Learning to play with the pros is a lesson which can take decades to sink in if a CEO tries to learn it on their own. An advisory board can shorten this learning process dramatically. Board members guide the team along the path towards professional status.

Forced Evolution

In the company that has reached the high teens in run rate,

the CEO may still have maintained the habit of acting as chief-of-everything. In order for the company to grow, this CEO must reinvent himself and serve his creation in an entirely different manner than was adequate during the early stages. So much of the activities which filled a normal day must be offloaded. An advisory board can accelerate this process and help the CEO navigate through a stressful time.

The CEO must become the company's senior business development officer. With the board in place, anywhere from half to three quarters of the CEO's time must be cleared for dealing with business development. That means the CEO needs to delegate significant responsibilities particularly in areas which are better served by others. For some CEOs this need can produce real stress. Board members who have managed the change in themselves are uniquely qualified to help others through the same process.

The Board tends to force this process of reinvention. In short order, the CEO will delegate all but the highest level of human resource supervision, most of the supervision of the accounting and financial controls, issues which surround the day to day physical functioning of the company and the process of maintaining quality control. All of this can seem pretty daunting if the CEO is making it up as he goes along. But with the help of advisers, his chances of successfully negotiating this process of re-invention and change management go up significantly.

These and other benefits accrue not so much because the advisers are kindly and supportive, but because they do not wish to risk their reputations on a company that is poorly organized, inadequately resourced or unprofessionally managed. The community of interest which evolves is based upon the strong self-interest of the advisers and the willingness of the senior management team to learn from them. This is admittedly a major challenge to the team but

84

one, if taken advantage of and overcome, can provide a significant edge over competition. Many of the CEOs I have built boards for have said that these ancillary benefits alone were worth the price of the board and the increased business is just gravy; albeit very valuable gravy.

High-Results Business Development

My discussion with a CEO or Chairman about designing, building and managing a board generally begins with an initial contact which has been the result of a recommendation by a friend or business associate. Most often the recommendation comes out of a discussion about the lack of effectiveness of the company's business development efforts or the revolving door that has become the company's business team. During the initial call I usually recommend that the person read several of my articles on advisory boards and then call back if they are still interested in talking.

I confess that I make this suggestion purely out of enlightened self-interest. I want to filter out the 'instant gratification' types who see the process of designing, populating and managing a productive advisory board as relatively simple and straightforward. If they will take the time to read and think about the articles, I take it as an indication that there is some hope that they are serious about engaging in ways that I have found necessary in order to produce a highly productive board that will drive the company's top line.

For those who call back there is yet another set of hurdles before we can discuss an engagement. I have learned that there is real benefit in running through a meticulous description of the process in person. It is important that the CEO or Chairman clearly understand what they are signing up for. Later is no time to realize.

What follows is a typical presentation in which I outline the dynamics of the process, a typical engagement and the areas that need to be thought through very carefully before embarking on the effort.

Parts of my presentation will vary with the size, complexity, scope and intensity of any engagement. But this should give you a fairly good idea as to what is involved. Assume that you and I are sitting in a comfortable place and that I am talking privately with you about advisory boards.

The Initial Message

One thing I have learned is that preparation is a critical part of the process. Another is that the company, and particularly the CEO, needs to have a good grasp on what is involved as well as what impact a board can have on the future of the company.

I'm not a golfer – never found a decent recipe for those little white balls – so I fish instead – but I'm told that a key to the game is preparation and practice. It is much the same with designing, populating and managing a board. I want to give you a fairly detailed briefing on what is involved.

First and foremost, this is an extended, complex and subtle process. You need to come to see that because sometimes tensions arise with CEOs who are anxious to get started. You may want to race through the 'getting ready' stage and get right to the 'getting people on your board' part. We need to slow down and get your mind around the process; so that you can understand clearly what is involved and we can lay the foundation that needs to be created before a board can be launched.

As a first step, we will need to make a baseline assessment. Your company is not ready for a board and there is much preparation necessary to get it ready. You may have built a company that is very good at doing what it does but managing and benefiting from a business development advisory board is something else again.

Building a board prior to completing the foundational work would be like dropping a Ferrari engine into a VW frame. Without a good bit of re-engineering, pop the clutch and you get a pretzel not a race car! This is what potential advisors would see and, in my experience, it is almost impossible to get high-potential members to make the kinds of commitments that a board requires if they see a train wreck as one of the likely future scenarios.

In the broader context, advisory boards are dangerous undertakings because the barriers to entry are so low. Any CEO can form one and most, at one time or another, try to. You could probably form one in an afternoon if you so decided. The trick is not getting a board set up. It is setting up a board that is highly productive when measured against a set of pre-established upon metrics. In this case the metrics are focused on driving the gross revenue of your company. They are very easy metrics to set up and monitor but harder ones to have a board meet.

Like most CEOs, you may suffer from several limitations that reduce your chances of success. First, although you are very good at the business of your business, your experience with highly productive boards, how to design, build and manage them, is limited. Second your range of contacts with potential members is also limited. My experience is that you need to contact close to twenty high-level candidates to fill one seat effectively on a board. Finally, you are very close to the trees and could use a set of eyes that is looking at the forest; a strategic view that can give you a holistic handle on the thing. An effective advisory board will impact, and place burdens on, every part of your company. But its members will also give you that long view that is so critical to your company's future success.

Here is something that you need to think about. We will eventually be dealing with very sophisticated, experienced, well connected individuals who have had careers that often involve building and managing businesses much larger than yours. They know good management when they see it. Most of them will have built and managed very successful teams. We will be asking them to risk their reputations by becoming strong advocates for your company; reputations that they have spent a lifetime carefully building. For them this is not just a consequential issue. It will be the central matter in their thinking. In every discussion they will be looking for indications that you and your team may drop the ball or not follow up effectively on the opportunities that they can bring to the table. They are very good at spotting those weaknesses. You will be dealing with pros at the top of their game.

Remember we are talking about building a board which will subject its members to a strict set of performance metrics. Members will be expected to produce. They will want to be sure that neither you nor the company, either through ineptness, inefficiency or poor organization and inadequate resourcing, will interfere with that performance. Simply saying that you 'won't' won't make any difference to them at all!

One of their security blankets will be the fact that you have brought in a set of professionals; a group of steady and experienced hands that they can trust. They have to buy into the model before they will be willing to place themselves on any particular board. Many of them will have had seats on non-productive boards. Most will have decided not to waste their time like that again. My presence in the process will give them confidence that the process is being approached professionally and with careful planning and execution.

The Risks of Going It Alone

After listening to all of this, you may decide to try this on your on – and if you do, *mazel tov*. But at least listen to what I have to say. It will help you assess the risks.

If you rush through this or do it badly, you will end up doing much damage to your company and its brand. Lots of CEOs have never thought of the negative branding that resulted from an unproductive board. But it is there and, the more influential your advisors are, the more broadly the negative branding will spread. That's right, the better the people you have on your board the more pervasive the consequences of screwing up. A couple of 'A' list advisors and a botched capture effort can turn your company into the proverbial 'dead man walking' long before your realize it. Even talking to very influential people has a severe downside if you haven't done the necessary spade work first.

A Typical Engagement

Let me outline the early stages of a typical engagement. Once an engagement agreement has been inked, we begin with a series of sessions in your office with you and your senior team. This stage has two principal objectives. The first is to thoroughly acquaint your team with advisory boards, the effort and commitment that will be required, the likely schedule that the engagement will follow, the relevant costs and benefits of the effort and to outline the terms and conditions of an extended engagement.

Secondly, I conduct a detailed assessment of your company, its history and resourcing and the potential benefits of building and managing a board for it. Successful graduation from this stage requires both that the company is ready to proceed with an engagement and I am convinced that the company is a good candidate for a board. This stage normally will take about a month to complete.

At the end of this phase, we begin an intensive effort of

creating a design for your board. I will work with your team to identify key targets for business expansion; both within existing business areas and into new ones. I will also work with other team members to rework your materials. This is particularly the case with the materials that will be presented to potential advisors and will be used by them in approaching targets. Very often CEOs have told me that this process alone results in a completely new understanding of their business and is a clear collateral benefit.

We complete a preliminary design for a tailor-made board, a description of the various seats on that board along with a profile of ideal members, a schedule for populating the board, cost estimates and a plan for the resourcing and reorganization that the company must undertake in order to prepare for the launch of the board. It normally takes two to three months to complete. So, you see we will have been at it for three or four months without talking to one potential advisor!

At the end of the first two steps, I will formally present my recommendations to you, members of your senior team, directors and other major stakeholders. Normally this is done within the context of a strategic planning retreat that covers other related areas critical to the process of actually designing, populating, launching and managing the board. The result of this step is an approved plan and an expanded engagement agreement.

Once the design of the board and the profiles of members are agreed on, I work to find candidates for each seat. Two to four candidates for each are normally identified - that's out of roughly twenty that will be contacted. Background information on each selected candidate will be presented to you and your senior team.

Once a candidate is approved, I arrange for interviews.

These interviews tend to be two-way streets with the company getting to know the candidate and the candidate getting to know the company and its senior team. Either can decide that discussions should not go forward at any point.

A major milestone in this process is when at least three board members have been identified, been offered and accepted seats and are ready to begin service. At this point we can launch of the board. The process of filling out a four to seven member board normally takes four to seven months.

While board seats are being filled, there is plenty that your team will need to be doing. It is vitally important that the company and senior management prepare for the launch and operation of the advisory board. This is not something that can be done 'on the run' or 'after the fact'. Board members who experience an unprepared team will quickly re-think their evaluation of the company and the risks to their reputation. The recommendations presented and agreed to during the strategic retreat must be implemented by your team prior to board launch.

Now we are getting close to the launch. Once a sufficient number of members have agreed to serve on the board, we will schedule and organize an initial meeting. I will handle the arrangements and facilitate the meeting. You and your team will undertake the substantial work that needs to be done in preparation. Generally it will take about a month to prepare for the meeting. The first meeting of any board is critical to its continued success.

I have found it a good idea to coordinate a first meeting with either a strategic planning retreat or an all-hands retreat. My experience in facilitating these meetings will go a long way to assuring that the board will be launched successfully and make major contributions to the company's future but your team will carry a substantial part of the burden.

Prior to the meeting, your team will have worked with each board member to identify targets of opportunity. It will be important that each member be involved in targeting at least one major source of business by the time the first meeting occurs.

A board normally meets four times a year. Two of the meetings are face-to-face. One of them coincides with your company's annual strategic planning while the other occurs roughly six months later. The other two meetings are normally teleconferences.

But most of the work of the board is done via direct contact between individual members and the company's senior team. Work, sometimes on a daily basis, with individual members to target, pursue and capture significant revenue opportunities will be your principal focus with the board. From my experience, you might end up spending as much as half to two-thirds of your time working with an active board. The percentages will be higher for your business development team.

While you and your team are working with board members, I will be managing the board. I will continually assess member's productivity, search for new members, advise you on the expansion of the board and on a whole range of other issues. We will facilitate meetings and conduct debriefings with each board member.

Summary

By the time the first session is over, you probably leave with lots to think about. Your senior team will be introduced to the idea of an advisory board.
My experience is that one in three CEOs decide, after such

an initial meeting, to continue discussions. Of the other two, half come back within six to nine months for the same purpose. The process filters out those who would not make good candidates.

Benefits and Costs

After thinking about our last meeting for a while, you will come back with a series of questions. They will probably be something like this:

o   What results should I expect from having a board and when should I start seeing them? What form will these benefits take and how will we be able to measure the value of them?

o   What will the board cost us to run and how should I put those costs in context? What are my fixed costs going to be? How about my variable costs? Could I really end up paying an advisor more than I pay anybody in the company – including me?

o   Tell me more about what changes we need to make in the company? What personnel changes am I going to have to make? How about resourcing changes? You mentioned that the culture of my company and focus on business development efforts will have to change – how and on what schedule?

o   What will be the demands on my time, my team's time and the resources of my company? It sounds like the board could take a lot of our time. How should I judge the wisdom of making this time and other resources available?

o   Tell me more about the ongoing management of the board. What areas will you be handling and why shouldn't we manage them? Is there going to be an end to the engagement?

o   What will it cost me to have you design, populate and manage a board? What are my upfront commitments? You mentioned an expanded engagement agreement. Under what conditions does that happen and how much more will it cost me?

These are all very good questions and I take them as an indication that we might be able to work together. It is time for the next session.

Some Necessary Preliminaries

Let's assume that we have reached an agreement for a preliminary engagement. Initially you might have wanted to meet at your office and involve some of your senior team. But I suggest that we have a couple of meetings one-on-one before involving others. That will give you a chance to get your mind around the process before introducing it to other members of your senior team. We agree on a second meeting. Here's how it might go:

You have obviously been doing a lot of thinking about advisory boards and our discussion. I suggest that we focus this session on two areas that you raised – the benefits and costs of having a board – and leave the others for later. My experience is that a more detailed description of the underlying value proposition will help you decide if further discussions are a good idea.

Before I launch into a description of the benefits, I need to cover some necessary preliminaries. These are issues that are so foundational to having an advisory board that, without your complete understanding of them, much of what we will do might be ineffectual. As we both want to avoid that outcome, let me quickly review four points.

First and foremost, real change is going to require real change and there is no way around it. By that I mean real change in the way you see the world and operate within it, the way your company is organized and resourced and the way your team functions just to name a few. You can't have a productive board and expect that the future will be just an extension of what you are already doing. In this case the past is prologue only in the extent that it will become a reference to the way you and your team used to operate.

Change needs to begin with you and members of your senior team. But it will affect everybody in your organization and you need not only to see the need for those changes but to accept and commit to them. They will go hand-in-hand with preparation for launch of the board. Effectively done, they will radically improve the chances of success. Poorly done, they will confuse your organization and turn the board into a liability. In short, things must change and your ability to manage these changes successfully will be a major factor in the benefits and costs calculation.

Second, part of the reorganization and resourcing that we will be doing will be focused on clearing the decks. An advisory board will require a great deal of time and attention from you and other members of your senior team. A board is not an ATM where you put in a code and take away money. But the time you spend with board members has the potential to generate returns that will drive your business to a new level. It will be time well spent.

You are going to have to clear a substantial part of your calendar for work with the board and the individual members. Your head of business development will have to as well. You should expect to spend as much as half your time working on developing the leads that they generate, overseeing the development, red-teaming and presentation of proposals and for meeting with individuals that members will want you to get to know. That percentage will increase dramatically when you are on the trail of a specific chunk of business.

The reorganization and resourcing work that we will be doing prior to launching the board will, in part, be focused on clearing the decks in preparation of the kind of action that the board will generate.

Third, we are going to design and implement a plan for shifting the focus of the current resourcing patterns within your company. You are not going to need the middle level business development types currently on your payroll. In many cases they will become more of a liability than an asset. You will have to step up your game substantially when it comes to preparation, red-teaming and presentation of proposals. And the capture process will have to work at a very high professional level. In short, we are going to have to prepare your company for the pressures that will come when the board shifts into high gear. Remember, the game is not getting opportunities; its winning business. That means closing on the target, bringing it down and dragging it back to camp for processing. Real winners manage the entire process seamlessly.

This resourcing plan will go farther than you might anticipate. We are going to have to look at the corporate infrastructure as well as sales and marketing. You will need the demonstrated ability to quickly and professionally expand your workforce, to keep track of rising levels of business and to manage accelerating change. A culture of professionalization is going to be necessary and it has to be in place before the board is launched. Potential board members will demand it.

Benefits

So now let's turn to some questions. Your first was "*What results should I expect from having a board and when should I start seeing them? What form will these benefits take and how will we be able to measure the value of them?*" These questions go to the heart of the value proposition of an advisory board. Let me go through the major benefits that your company will realize as a result of successfully taking advantage of a board.

I'll start with an intangible benefit; branding. Yes, there is major benefits in having recognizable names on your board and that is a type of branding alright. But it is a different matter altogether when influential individuals are willing to aggressively represent your company to decision makers. Your company immediately steps up to a different level. You should start seeing these benefits as soon as you kick off the publicity campaign to announce the board. The more coverage you get that links these influential people to your company the better. You should notice an increased level of interest and improved brand recognition among the decision makers you are brought in contact with.

Second, board members will be bringing you opportunities to capture new business that you would not normally have. Those opportunities will represent larger chunks of business which will help you to accelerate your rate of growth. You should start seeing these opportunities begin to fill your pipeline in the early months after board launch.

Additionally, board members will help you expand existing areas of business. You will start to get more out of the beachheads that you have already established. You should see an improvement in prospects in established areas of business almost immediately.

Each board member should be targeting at least one major source of business prior to launch. While it will take a while to completely fill, you should see your pipeline begin to fill up with larger chunks of potential new business. Monitoring this flow - particularly the velocity of deals through the pipeline - will give you an idea as to how well the board is performing.

Third, you will be brought in contact with a wider and more powerful set of contacts. Remember that board members will have had very successful careers prior to joining your board. Part of their contribution will be bringing you and your company in contact with influential individuals and organizations which will help you grow.

You and your team will need to manage these new contacts very professionally. Some of them will be sources of the proverbial low-hanging-fruit while others will take longer to develop into sources of business. But you will need to spend part of your time cultivating these relationships; in close concert with the board members, of course. You can keep track of the expansion of the range and increase in quality of your contacts and the contacts of your senior team.

Forth, you will gain a group of strong and influential advocates. Board members will be acting as advocates not just introducers. Your ability to work with them and effectively take advantage of the doors that they will be opening will be tested in the early stages. The first set of metrics will focus on how well you and your team are establishing those relationships but later on, once you have mastered that process, they will shift to how well you and your team are converting initial contacts to productive, working relationships. The board should be an ongoing source of an expanding network of highly productive relationships.

Fifth, you should see a more effective targeting, proposal development, red-teaming, capture and processing of new business. That means that your company should be pursuing larger and higher quality opportunities. But that's only the beginning. You should see a radical improvement in the quality of your proposals and a higher win rate. Your proposals should be more effectively targeted to the needs of the potential client.

Sixth, you and your team will benefit from the wisdom and mentoring which will take place because of your close contact with board members. Remember, these individuals will have successfully build and run organizations much larger than yours. They will have experiences that goes beyond yours and those of your senior team. Their combined judgments and wisdom can be a resource of incalculable value to you and your team. It will be up to you to take advantage of this resource.

Finally, a well managed and productive board will be seen as a significant asset when it comes to valuation of your company. When we get to the point of talking about exit strategies, the fact that you have influential individuals who are committed to effective advocacy will be seen as a major plus by any strategic buyer.

Costs

Now let's turn to your questions about the costs of running a board. *"What will the board cost us to run and how should I put those costs in context? What are my fixed costs going to be? How about my variable costs? Could I really end up paying an advisor more than I pay anybody in the company – including me?"*

So let me outline the various costs associated with designing, populating and managing an advisory board. Let's start with the planning phase. I charge a retainer for the design, population and management of an advisory board. Costs are going to vary depending on size, complexity and intensity of the board required.

A typical retainer would be somewhere between two and four thousand per month for the early, planning stages and four to eight thousand per month for the latter stages.

The first phase of our engagement will involve two stages. The first stage will continue until the advisory board has been designed and a plan for work within your company has been agreed on. That plan will include issues like resourcing, expansion of your team and revisions of materials. At the end of this phase we will present our findings and recommendations.

The end products of the planning stage will be a design for the board, a detailed description of each board seat and profile of the ideal member and a plan for getting you and your team ready for the board. The planning stage usually takes between two and three months.

Once we have completed this stage we will begin the implementation phase. We will begin the search for board members and you and your team, with my help, will begin the process of preparing you, your team and company. I can't make the point too strongly, it is going to be critical that you and your team implement the plan that we agree on. That implementation is usually the critical path.

I will identify a list of candidates for each board seat. I will conduct the necessary background checks and acquaint the candidates with your company. In some cases we will ask you or members of your team to meet with candidates. This is a process of getting acquainted and it is definitely a two way street.

It's going to take a minimum of six to seven months to complete the plan and identify the candidates for your board. Once we have at least three board members, we will begin planning for the first board meeting. The second stage of our engagement ends with that first meeting.

Now let's talk about how board members get compensated. Members will receive a retainer, an honorarium for meeting attendance and a reimbursement of out-of-pocket expenses. In general, and for a board of six members, the total costs in these categories will amount to what you pay one middle-level business development type. That's right, six high powered advocates for the cost of one middle-level employee.

The biggest part of board members compensation will result from their incentivized compensation agreement. They will receive payments that are calculated based on the dollar amounts of revenue they are instrumental in helping the company capture. That means that they receive payments only if you actually win new business. The more new business they bring in, the more they will get paid. So to answer one of your questions directly, yes you could end up paying a member significantly more than you earn in any given year. But I think you will be able to live with that. You will want them to do it again and again won't you?

For board members who serve longer than one year I generally recommend that you offer them a chance to build a small equity stake in the company. This is generally in the form of warrants or options. It is nothing major but I have found that it generates a sense of loyalty to the company and will be seen as a recognition of their value contribution.

So that's how the board members get paid. To wrap this up, here is how I get paid on an ongoing basis. I serve on each board that I construct. I am responsible for the board's smooth operation, the assessment of member effectiveness, replacement of ineffective members and the expansion of the membership. For this service, I receive the standard board member compensation package – but no incentivized compensation agreement. In addition, I receive a retainer for an ongoing search for new members; either to replace existing members or to expand the board.

Well, that's it. I'm sure that you will have questions about what I've told you. I suggest that we gather again and this time focus on the balance of your questions. I also suggest that we focus on what it will be like to work with the board and how your world will be different.

Branding and Board Management

Let's say we scheduled a third session to discuss the balance of your questions and the changes that will be necessary within your company to accommodate and take advantage of having a board. This is how it might go:
Last time we discussed the benefits and costs of an advisory board. I want to give you some time to ask any questions that have come up as a result. Then I want to move to the balance of the questions you posed after our initial lunch.

Questions

I appreciate your time and patience. Mostly consultants try to close a deal during the first meeting with a high-pressure sales job that I tend to resent. I appreciate that you are taking a different approach. After our first two sessions, I am beginning to see why you are cautious about entering into engagements. This is major surgery and the patient clearly has to be very healthy, eager for the procedure, understand what is involved and be ready and able to make the necessary commitments.

One thing has stood out in my mind. You said that "real change requires real change." At first I admit that I thought it was just a trick with words but the longer I thought about it the truer it came to seem. We will not be playing around the edges with an advisory board and all parts of my company will be affected by having one.

I've thought quite a bit about what it would be like to have five or six very well connected and successful people on the board. I understand why you spent so much time on this. These people are going to expect me to have time for them and to follow up on the opportunities that they can provide. You're right, I will have to clear my decks and prepare for

104

this.

I also understand something of what you were getting at when you said that the culture of my team and company needs to be professionalized. I had drinks with a friend who is part of the senior business development team of a large company. They have an advisory board that does something similar to your version.

He told me that the board was a source of substantial new business on a regular basis. Then he started to sound like you. He said that most of his time is spent interacting with board members, following up on their introductions and shepherding the responses. He admitted that, at first, he underestimated the time requirements and tried to operate on a business-as-usual basis. But one of the board members backed him up against the wall and explained the world to him.

But the second thing he said, and this is the one I wanted to mention, was that the member told him in no uncertain terms that his proposal development, red-teaming, presentation and capture resourcing was totally inadequate and that he had better step up his company's game ASAP; before he embarrasses himself and board members.

I took that as a serious bit of information – I still remember the look on his face as he said it. They almost lost their entire board over this.

Finally, I now recognize that the changes in resourcing within my team and company will have to be pervasive and necessary for supporting and taking advantage of a board. I don't see the details of the changes at this point but I do see their general outlines and understand that they will be necessary prior to actually launching the board.

Branding

Oh yes, let's start with branding. I understand what you are saying about improved branding but how does my company take advantage of it? We are a private company that is not affected by public opinion so public relations is not something we spend much time on.

Good question. The branding that I am talking about is focused on the decision makers who directly affect the chances of your company winning new business. Most CEOs and almost all PR firms focus in an unfocused way on too broad an audience. Branding is important if it helps to facilitate a positive outcome of a decision that really matters.

Managing the Board

OK, I'll accept that. You said that the board will be a source of "opportunities to capture new business" that we would not normally have. How will that work?
The identification of new opportunities will be the focus of board meetings and a good part of your time with individual members. You will be leveraging the members contacts and reputation. Their willingness to make introductions and act as advocates will be critical to the success of the board.

But, remember that a board and its members do not constitute an ATM. You are going to have to work to build relationships based on trust. The stronger the relationships the more and higher quality the opportunities that will result.
I'll buy that. I sometimes wonder if my team and I will be good enough to earn that trust.

You can't cower in the shadow of the board. You will need to find the stiffness to engage with these people and set expectations, metrics and drive the agenda. Believe me they will expect it and be disappointed if you don't. The short answer is that you and your team have *to become good enough if this is going to work.*

Also remember that nobody will accept an invitation to join your board unless they are convinced that you and your team are up to the challenge. The mere fact that you have a populated board will be an indication that at least they think you are worth the effort and exposure
.

OK, that's a bit daunting in and of itself. Let's move on. I accept your suggestion that my company will become exposed to "a wider and more powerful set of contacts". I also buy into the proposition that the board will constitute "a set of strong and influential advocates". The kinds of people you have described and the way the relationship with each of them is to develop virtually guarantees that. I understand that converting these assets into new business will require "a more effective targeting, proposal development, red-teaming, capture and processing of new business." I hope that we can talk a bit about what that means.

Before that, I want to visit two other points that you made. You said that one benefit would be the "wisdom and mentoring" that I and my team would have access to. Could you say a bit more about that? Also, you mentioned the effect of the board on valuation. We are not planning to exit anytime soon, but valuation is something that I think about. Could you say a bit more about how a board will affect it?

First, mentoring relationships have evolved within all the boards that I have constructed. Most members are in what I call a grandfatherly mode, meaning that they value the chance to give back to the next generation the lessons that they have learned. If you are open to it, at least one of the members will begin to work with you on your management style and decision making. Others may partner with your business development team to help them raise their game. It happens naturally enough and is an additional benefit; one you receive just by being in contact with the kinds of people we put on a board and are open to receiving their help.

Valuation is a matter of perception as much as the numbers. You have to see your company through the eyes of a strategic buyer not an accountant. A company that has attracted the kinds of people that would be on your board and has negotiated the pro-active understandings with them that go with such a board will be seen as having significantly more value than one that has an ordinary, mostly unproductive advisory board. The latter is almost always taken as an indication of failed management with appropriate discounts applied.

That's what I thought you would say. It is up to us to make this work. I remember you once saying that "you can lead a horticulture but you can't make her think." It's going to be up to us, my team and me, to think and act; to realize the value that is there to create.

Lets deal with your earlier question about more effective targeting, proposal development, red-teaming, capture and processing of new business. How are you and your team going to have to change the way you are doing business?

Your larger competitors have a highly developed process for identifying business that they want to pursue. You need to begin to emulate them. Targeting will be more focused on the core competencies of your company; what you are really good at. You will need to start sifting out the good targets from the red-herrings much more aggressively and effectively.

These competitors also have a more finely tuned proposal development and red-teaming process. Your team needs to up its game in these areas. You will need to play like the pros and deliver like them as well. One early advantage of the board will be that you will have a resource to guide you in this process. But you must make significant progress on the evolution of the corporate culture and capabilities before the board can be launched. Members will expect that you recognize the difference between what you have been doing and what you need to do to compete more effectively.

One of the principal challenges of winning larger chunks of business will be getting the organization up to speed to actually deliver. We will be focusing on the infrastructure; those areas which are critical to your company's ability to do that. There will be greater stress on human resources during major ramp-ups. Your accounting and reporting systems will need to be looked at. Contract compliance, which you are already pretty good at, will have to be beefed up. I think that you get the idea.

I am beginning to. Let's talk about the process you outlined. You described a planning period and described it as getting ready for having the board. It involved designing the board and developing a detailed description of each seat on the board and the ideal occupants. As I remember, you said that would take between two and three months. My team and I are anxious to get going on this. Isn't there some way to shorten the planning period?

I'd like to say that there is but I would be misleading you. This is a complex process that requires careful planning and extended focus. SWAGs are not going to do anything but get you in trouble. And that's what you end up with if you try to phone in or short-circuit the planning process.

One of the most time consuming parts of this stage will be designing and implementing plans for refocusing your company. There may be significant changes required in your management team. Most often we end up adding very experienced people in key areas. There will be new support systems to put in place. Your CRM will have to be beefed up, for instance. And all of these systems will have to be tested before launch of the board.

As I mentioned in the last session, almost all of the materials that you now use in your business development efforts will have to be reviewed and most will probably have to be revised.

Well that was sobering! I know that you have said these things before but that certainly got my attention. I think that I am beginning to realize how big a change this is going to be and why you are constantly counseling caution. Ok, let's say that it is going to take three months although now I suspect maybe more. How much time are we going to need from my team and how do we go about organizing them?

You are always going to underestimate the time required. For these two to three months you should think in terms of a dominating agenda. That means that you are going to have to let your people in on the process you are going through, tell them about the board and why it will be important to the company and get their buy-in to supporting the process by helping to clear up your calendar. In the long term this will be therapeutic beyond just this project. Letting people in and asking for their help should be a major part of your management style.

Once you have made the arrangements for clearing your calendar you will need to meet with other senior members of your team. They will need to be briefed on the approach and their commitments to the process will be a key to its success. For them, as well as you, it's going to be immersion learning. Figure that this will dominate their lives as well as yours for the foreseeable future. We need to get it right and the only way I know to do that is to bear down and focus.

Once we begin to get the outlines of the board and reorganization plan, things will get even more complicated. We will begin to involve others in your company. That circle will grow until virtually everybody is involved.

Sounds like a pretty intense two to three months.

It will be; more intense than you can know. But we are talking about the very future of your company and everybody connected with it. You and your team will be stretched and challenged. This is strategic stuff.

Costs Comparison

You talked about the relative costs of having a board. The fixed costs about at the level of one middle-level business development type as I recall. What will be the impact of the board on the company? Will it cost us more or less to do business development this way?

It will cost you more. But not as much more as you might think. You will replace the middle-level business development types with a board. You will also beef up your targeting, proposal development, red-teaming and capture resources. There will be investments in new systems and the process of getting everybody up to speed. Your calculation needs to be a cost/benefit one. The question is "if I make the investment in a board, will it pay off?" Now before you look for a quick answer to that question, we will need to get through the planning phase.

Changing The Roles

You have said more than once that I will have to change my approach to the CEO role. What do you mean by that?

111

Change in an organization comes either with the leadership of the founders or over their dead bodies. Organizations that need to grow always prefer that the head person lead the charge. The problem gets even more severe when you set on a course like building and managing an advisory board. My boards are not only powerful business development engines; they are also powerful agents for change within a corporate culture.

The biggest initial stresses come on the senior management. You and your team cannot continue to do business as you have. Delegation becomes a key skill. The strength of your judgment about people sits at the very center of the process. You must pick the right people for the right slots and then leave them to do what they are skilled to do. Micro-management will go out the window or you will go out with it. The days of dabbling in human resources or financial reporting or quality control will be gone.

You must come to see your company in a larger vision and your role in it in a narrower and more focused one. As a CEO you can no longer be 'chief-of-everything'. Your leadership will focus more on choosing the right people and making sure that they have the resources for success. So you will become part quarterback and part water boy!

And what of my team - how will all of this affect them?

Those that can grow with the company, meet the needs to professionalize the culture and their performance, will survive and thrive. Others will decide that they are more suited for the relatively open but higher risk environment of a start-up and will depart for what they see as greener pastures. Some may fight the process and need to be shown the door; insisting to the end that you have sold out the very soul of your company. The thing about other people, is that you don't get to write their lines; only your own. Your task will be to give them every chance and help to make the transition.

Change Management

I hope we have covered the questions that you had as a result of our last session. Let's move on to the balance of the questions.

o   Tell me more about what changes we need to make in my company. What personnel changes am I going to have to make? How about resourcing changes? You mentioned that the culture of my company and focus of our business development efforts will have to change; how and on what schedule?
o   What will be the demands on my time, my team's time and the resources of my company? It sounds like the board could take a lot of our time.
o   Tell me more about the ongoing management of the board. What areas will you be handling and why shouldn't we manage them? Is there going to be an end to the engagement?

Personal Growth

Let's start by talking about the changes that you are going to have to manage within your company. Remember my maxim – real change requires real change. You can simulate real change by simply moving the flatware around on the table but the effort will turn out to be a kamikaze raid on a vacant lot. The kind of changes that I am talking about are fundamental and strategic – purely tactical or virtual responses will only derail the process.
What do you mean by that?

Your overall goal is to grow your company and that involves seeing to the process of its maturing. Think of your company as your child. It is growing up before your eyes and you are doing your very best to see that it gets what it needs to grow in healthy and empowering ways. Now it needs to develop more of its own persona and become a young adult.

Perhaps you have never thought of yourself as the parent of your company.

In a foundational way you are. As a parent, you have been responsible for keeping your company on the upward path, protecting it from its own excesses - seeing that it matures into a young adult that is widely recognized as a productive and welcomed member of society. Think of this process in two parts – efforts to make your company the best it can be and efforts to make it a very productive and well accepted member of the larger community of companies.

Your company needs to develop the maturity that comes with age and experience. Its internal culture will evolve and expand to include skills and resources that were not particularly important in the early years. Other tendencies will be put away as remnants of a more child-like time. And your role as parent needs to evolve also. You won't be able to make all the decisions any more – a real crisis for most parents!

Simpler days brought lots of work that others now do. Now you sometimes feel like you are losing control – or, worse, becoming irrelevant.

You are in a way losing control – but also gaining new control at the same time. You can't be relevant in the terms you used to be. The company has grown beyond that. You can't relate to a teenager in the same way as you did to a three year old. But the new relationship can be richer and far more satisfying to both.

As I mentioned before, the existence of an advisory board tends to accelerate the maturation of any organization. A board populated by very experienced, successful and well-connected individuals comes with a lot of direct experience with that 'mature culture' that your company needs to develop. Members will naturally expect the company to meet the dual standards of a mature individual and a productive member of corporate society.

The initial test comes as board members get to know you and your team. They will not expect you to be ready to run a major company. If you were, you would be. But they will pay particular attention to your efforts to grow your capabilities in that direction.

Members will judge not only who you are but who you are trying to become and your chances of successfully making the journey. Their willingness to expand their commitments to you and the team will be guided by their conclusions in these areas.

So, I and my team are on trial from the very beginning.

Let's not say 'on trial'. Maybe 'on probation' is a better term. Remember that these individuals will have made a decision to join your board – and that in itself is a substantial vote of confidence.

To be as direct as I can, you will be on probation and the judges will be vastly more experienced and knowledgeable about what it is going to take for your company to succeed. If you are all ego and smoke, they will flush the toilet and move on - mostly in disgust. If you pass muster, they will support you and begin to bring you the opportunities that are the underlying purpose of the board.

Board members will also be getting to know your senior team. It will be important that you set the tone for those relationships – leading by example. Your team members will watch how you interact with the board and how determined you are to grow personally. You need that determination to become contagious!

You said a couple of times that I will have to be ready for major changes in your team. What did you mean by that?

When a company was in the early stages of growth you often have little to incentivized people with. Money was tight, equity is illiquid and career tracks are narrow and short. So most people in your position give titles – it is all there was that might mean something to the recipient. But there is a downside to this strategy and it starts to show up when growth complicates the challenges that each team member must manage.

Let's look at human resources. In your early years your VP of human resources could be a highly effective recruiter – in fact, that was probably the most effective strategy. But, as the company grew, the challenges that must be dealt with got not only much more complex but also much more potentially damaging if mismanaged. I believe that you are working through your first equal opportunity lawsuit, aren't you?

We sure are – and it's a real pain. I can relate to your point. It's becoming clear that our VP of human resources is not up to the challenge. We have had to get lawyers involved across a much broader range of issues than I would have thought. The costs are running up fast. It seems we have not been in compliance with a bunch of requirements. The complaint is specious but our failure to cover key bases is coming back to bite us in the butt.

Sorry to hear that. If it helps, I have heard it before.
Doesn't much – but thanks anyway.

Another position that is often a problem as a company grows is that of VP of Finance. In the early years a controller was fine. But, as things get more complicated and start to come in faster and in larger chunks, things can get out of hand for less experienced people. I know that you have been bringing in a part-time CFO. How's that working out?

The difference has been noticeable almost from the very beginning. I had no idea that things had gotten so badly out of whack. But a couple of months of working with our new VP of Finance has brought things along. He needs to learn in order to be a real vice president of finance. He has decided to go back to school and we've agreed to foot the bill.

A very wise decision. You should give him and people like him every support if they are determined to grow with the job. Some of your people won't make the journey with you. Others will, and you should support them.

Resourcing

Now let's move on to the question of resourcing. As I mentioned before, you will need to change some of the resourcing patterns within your company. For one thing, you will not have to spend so much on your junior-level business development team. But you will have to increase investments in proposal development, red-teaming and capture.

One suggestion that I have is that you need to review the performance and qualifications of your head of business development. I'm not sure you have the right person in that slot. Remember, I said 'not sure'. Clearly there has been significant success in that area. I recommend that I spend some time with that person and give you my recommendations.

I think I have a pretty clear picture in this area. I have

already started to think about how to make the changes. I'll admit that it seemed pretty daunting at first but, once I sat down and got my mind around it, the planning went much better.

Good – I'm glad that you are working that set of challenges. Some of our heaviest lifting in the early stages will be developing and implementing a plan for reorganizing your company and getting it ready for the board.

Cultural Changes

Last time we talked about how the company's culture was going to professionalize. Do you think that you have a handle on that?

I'm not sure. I've been talking about 'professionalization' with some of my friends. I've sure gotten a range of reactions from them. Some see the point immediately and talk about how I need to let it happen and up my game to keep pace. Others look at me with something approaching horror and end up asking 'how could you let that happen to a great company like mine?'

As you know, I talk to lots of people about major challenges that I'm facing. I've found that it helps me get a clearer picture of the options and better choose the right path. But this one is all over the map. Why is it that the very idea of professionalizing a corporate culture seems to draw such a range of reactions?

There is an ancient Chinese proverb that might help here. Among all dragonfly larva there is a blood oath that the next one that goes through the barrier will come back and tell the others what it is like. But it has never happened. Why?

Probably because dragonfly larvae live in water and when

they cross the barrier they become air breathing insects.

Yes, that's right. The larvae cannot live in air – it is a mortal threat to them. But neither can a dragonfly live in water. What was once a sustaining environment is now a death trap. Some people live their lives avoiding the process of professionalization. For them the very thought of such an environment is threatening. Others have made the journey across the barrier and the very thought of a less-than-professional culture offends their sensibilities. You can tell a lot about somebody by engaging them on this issue.

But, that aside, you have to decide whether you are willing to allow your company's culture to professionalize.

You once said to me that "change in an organization either occurs with the support of the founders or over their dead bodies". I've thought about it and have decided that I would rather survive the process.

Time Commitments

That decision alone – if you can stand by it – is a major advance. Now let's talk about time commitments. You asked "What will be the demands on my time, my team's time and the resources of my company?" The initial stages of the planning process are going to be very time consuming. We will need to be methodical in our analysis and planning. You are right to conclude that, once up and operating, the board will take a lot of your time. Investment of time in the process will yield benefits in proportion to your ability to make that time available and to constructively and creatively engage with the board.

We will have to pay a lot of attention to adjusting the load within your company. We don't want to simply pile more onto the backs of you and your senior team. It's not just the time commitments of your senior team that you need to pay attention to. We will need to shift some burdens onto the desks of others. Delegation of responsibility and authority is going to be a big part of the process and a major focus of our planning.

A lot of time will have to go into explaining the process and its implications to key people. We will need buy-in from those people who are going to have to pick up delegated responsibilities. We will need to help them understand what is going on and why their world is changing so much. All of this needs to be put into the context of your vision for your company.

And what about the demands of our resources – particularly capital resources?

Building a board is a lot like planting a crop. As I said before, an advisory board is not an ATM – where you put in a code and get back cash. You will be forward investing in the board – just like a farmer prepares the field, adds fertilizer, plants the seeds and tends the field. The success of any board depends on how well you engage in each of these activities – how good you and your team are at farming.

Your investment will be in the cost of the engagement, the time invested by you and your team and the costs of materials and events that are associated with the process of designing, setting up, populating and managing the board. In addition, because there will be a sales cycle involved, you will have to carry the board until the first revenue check clears.

The decision to launch a board is a calculated one based on a judgment that initial investments will yield very substantial benefits down the road. Advisory boards are not for those insisting on instant gratification.

OK – let's move to the final set of questions. You wanted to hear more about my ongoing management of the board.

We have found that, particularly in the early years, it is a good idea for me to stay involved in the management of the board. There are six major areas that we work in.

The first is the facilitation of the developing relationship between the board and your team. It is important that this goes well. It sets the tone of much of what is to follow – it either limits or expands the potential of the board. My participation as a facilitator and honest broker will help you and the board members navigate the shoals and reefs of the early months. If a disagreement arises, I will mediate.

Second, I provide the organizing center of the board. I communicate with members about how things are going and whether their expectations are being met. In this role I can serve as a kind of early warning sensor net – getting you and your team information about stresses that are developing or opportunities that are being missed.

Third, during the first year I chair the board meetings. I make sure that the agendas are well formed, that each member is contributing. My participation helps you and your team to learn to handle the process of managing the board.

Fourth, I facilitate review and training sessions for your team focused on how to work with the board. I also identify issues as they arise and work with all parties to resolve them. My objective is to give you a smoothly working and highly productive advisory board and to help you learn how to maximize your returns from it.

Fifth, I lead the process of assessing the performance and contributions of each board member. I arrange for replacements in the event that one is needed.

Sixth, I take the lead in expansion of the board. When we get to the point of adding seats, I will identify and qualify additional board members.

Board Management

As I recall your last question was "What areas will you be handling and why shouldn't we manage them? Is there going to be an end to the engagement?" Well, to answer the last question first, my involvement will end the moment that you feel we are not adding value to the process substantially in excess of the cost of that engagement. I am always aware that the decision to continue is yours.

I do insist that your company commit to an initial period without reservation. But at any time after that you can simply end the engagement by notifying me. My belief is that I need to be generating so much value that you will not even think of saving the money and spending it somewhere else. I am dedicated to being the highest return on investment that you make.

I manage your board on an ongoing basis for three reasons. The first is based on my experience with many companies and boards. Preparing a management team for dealing with the board is an art. We have seen normally confident CEOs go into vapor lock when confronted with a board. The stakes are simply too high to trust that process to fate or chance.

Secondly, I have a different relationship with board members. I can have conversations with board members that would be hard for you and your team. My approach can be more direct.

123

Finally, I can maintain a strategic, top-down view, of the battlefield. I bring a perspective into the mix that is from above the fray.

Engagement

Well, that's it in a nutshell. You have the whole crop. Nothing left but to decide. Here is an agreement for our initial engagement. You'll notice that it is only one page long. Take a read through it. When you are ready to go, sign it and send a copy back to me.

Let's assume that, after taking a few minutes to read it through, you sign the agreement and hand it back.

"I'm ready to go. You'll have your first check delivered in the morning. Let's plan a kick-off session for next week."

The Board – Design and Population

Producing a well-balanced design for a board is part science and part art - but it is mostly science and serious spade work. Board seats should be a reflection of the company's current strengths and future business development aspirations. The board should also be proportional to the company's capabilities. By that I mean that a three or four seat board might be all one company can handle while a six or seven person board would be manageable for another. Finally, the levels of reputation, experience, range of connections and activity of board members should be designed into it. A board should be tailor-made to a company's capabilities. One size definitely does not fit all.

The Design

The easiest way to begin the design of a board is to start with a detailed review of a company's client base. Particular attention needs to be paid to the potential for expansion of the beachheads that have already been established. Areas should be identified that show potential for extensive growth. Board seats should be designed around these areas and support and extend the company's business development efforts. Seats should also be allocated to areas where the company is looking to expand – either in terms of new clients with existing products or services or entirely new additions to the product/service mix.

We start by identifying the most logical seats that a board should have. Each is described in terms of an existing client base, sales channel or product/service. These are the areas that the member will be asked to help with. In some companies this will be a particular segment of a government agency. In others it might be a type of sales channel. The goal is to rough out an initial design based on these areas.

Once the rough design is in place, we set about refining it. It is important to get the descriptions of the focus of each seat as detailed as possible. We develop a careful description of the knowledge, connections and reputation that an ideal board member would have. As these descriptions evolve we constantly visit questions of the depth and balance of the evolving board design, the characteristics of the ideal members and how we would actually stand-up the board – prepare for the launch and select board members.

Ideal Members

There are lots of people who would jump at a chance to serve on an advisory board. Most will either be unqualified or incapable of meeting their responsibilities. Many do it because they consider it good for their resume. Others because the think that the board is going to be some sort of coffee clutch – a senior advisory committee. We regularly encounter wanna-bee CEOs who see the board as their chance to prove to the world that they know how to run a company. But these boards are not honorary and they are not advisory in that sense. Board members are expected to generate actual leads to significant chunks of business. They are required to be effective advocates for the company in the process of capturing business and they will be measured by a strict set of metrics which are based on their productivity. That means that they have to be the principal reason that a company gets a high quality shot at significant pieces of new business. If they don't perform they will be removed.

Ideal board members have five major characteristics. The first and foremost is that they clearly understand and accept the obligations that they will be assuming as part of the advisory board. I can't emphasize this too strongly. This understanding must be reached from the very first conversations with a potential board member. Later is too late.

Second, the potential member may be retired but it is important that they are not retiring. By that I mean that they may have left full time participation in an organization in exchange for a more flexible schedule but they should not be deciding how much work and how much golf - with the golf increasingly winning out. The ideal board member is a highly active and motivated individual who wants to make a difference.

Third, the reputation of a board member is always their strongest asset. The individual should not only be widely known in a space but widely respected as well. They should be able to leverage that reputation in service to the company. Their highest focus should be its welfare. And they should not be seen as trying to monetize their reputation gratuitously. If their advocacy is seen as reflexively instrumental they probably should move into politics where that is the norm.

Forth, an ideal board member has a wide range of currently active contacts in the space that they are going to be targeting. This is one of those areas that need to be checked very carefully. Some contacts have a very short shelf-life.

Others stay fresh for years.

Finally, it is important that the potential member be willing and able to make the kinds of commitments that participation will require. Board members need to be able to work closely with the senior team. They will be participating in a complex process of engagement, targeting, and capture and delivering on important pieces of business. Members will be asked to be supportive of others on the board. In short, they need to clearly understand what is going to be involved and just as clearly capable and willing to fill the role.

The Search

The heart of an effective search for board members is a well-constructed network of senior recruiters and other people of influence. The net needs to be very widely flung on the one hand and very well focused on the other. Our experience is that we look at preliminary information on a hundred potential members to identify just one. That alone should give you a good idea of what we go through just to populate a six or seven seat board.

Of course, recruiters are not primarily in the business of filling board seats. There isn't enough money in it to make the effort cost effective and often the candidates are rather hard to find. Over the years we have developed broader-based relationships with recruiters which allow us to be more effective in the search.

It is critical that the search be both extensive and effective. Getting the right candidates and negotiating the right understanding with them is the key to populating the board. The work is hard and sometimes frustrating. But this is no place for an easy way out.

The search process is also a major source of uncertainty when it comes to the time required to stand up a board. It takes as much time as it takes and we have to understand and accept that. At times we get lucky and completely fill out a board in a couple months. At other times we are still searching for the right person for a particular seat months later. The best we can do is to make sure the search is well based and designed and that we are diligently following every lead that is generated.

One major advantage that we have is that a growing number of recruiters now already know the basic requirements of service on a Longview advisory board. This institutionalized knowledge is invaluable as it allows them to pre-screen candidates. Some recruiters have increased their hit rate from one in a hundred to one in ten! You can imagine how much easier they are to deal with.

Identifying and Vetting Candidates

Once candidates have been identified the process of prioritizing and vetting begins. In many ways it is similar to vetting a potential member of the senior team. We are very interested in learning about the person – their skills, reputation, integrity, range of contacts, capabilities, intentions and suitability. We are also concerned that they understand very clearly what is going to be expected of them and that they are ready, willing and able to make the kinds of commitments that are required.

We conduct initial interviews and the early screening on behalf of the company. We start with a traditional CV. Our next step is to identify those people who, based on that information, would seem to be good candidates. We then deliver an extensive package to them which includes information on the company, a description of the board, information on board membership – compensation – responsibilities and a package outlining the terms of engagement. We ask them to review the materials in anticipation of a teleconference. The call is designed to answer any of their questions about the company, the board and their responsibilities as members. The experience is illuminating in many ways. Somewhere around a third of the candidates decide not to go any further at this point. It may be the first time that they come to realize that membership on an advisory board will be real work – and that is not what they are looking for. They may just decide that it will be too much work – taking too much time from golf. Or they may decide that, after years of calling the shots, they are not prepared to work in an advisory role and be subject to performance metrics. For whatever reason, they drop out of consideration.

For those that do survive this initial conference we call for references and engage them in conversations about the specific seat on the board that they would be invited to occupy. This phase involves the execution of a non-disclosure agreement (NDA) because considerably more detail is provided about the company and its relationships with existing clients. The candidate is asked to develop a plan for supporting the company's efforts to capture new business in specific areas. This plan focuses heavily on the connections that the candidate has and the possibility that they will be useful to the efforts. We use these plans as the basis for selecting candidates for meetings with the company's senior team.

Filling Out the Board

By the time we have identified a number of candidates we have substantial files on them. Our next step is to meet with the senior team and go through all the files. The meeting agenda involves a careful consideration of each one. The result of that meeting is a prioritization of the candidates and a list of additional information which the team needs to get ready for actually meeting with them. By the end of the session we will have a set of additional questions to pass on to the candidates.

The first introductions come when individual candidates are invited to meet with the CEO, COO and/or SVP Business Development. Most of the time these meetings are face-to-face. We very occasionally use video-conferencing when schedules are tight and distances great. My own preference is that these first meetings be quasi-social. They tend to be casual and without highly structured agendas.

Everybody already knows the basics of what they need to know about each other. It is now a process of filling in the blanks and gauging the chemistry. Much of the time is spent on 'how well do you know x' or 'what do you know about the y program' – and these conversations tend to flow in both directions. By the end of the meeting both sides generally have decided whether they can and want to work together. Our hit rate during this phase is very high – better than two-thirds of the candidates both pass muster and decide to go to the next phase of discussions. Of the other third by far the majority of them withdraws rather than is declined.

Generally there will be a minimum of two to three meetings with each candidate before an offer of a board seat is extended. These meetings will tend to focus on the candidates plan for supporting the company and the integration of that plan into the company's business development efforts. If things go well, the result will be an offer of a seat.

We go through this process for each seat on the board. Multiply the number of meetings and the work required for one seat by six or seven – and then factor in that again for null results - and you will get an idea of how much is involved.

A major milestone occurs when we have at least three board seats filled. At that point we can begin to organize an initial meeting. It is time to stand up the board.

Now let's return to our narrative. The board has been in existence for about six months. We are about to deal with a major problem – the removal of a board member.

The First Board Meeting

Let's say that three members have signed on. That means that we can organize the very first board meeting. It also means that the senior team has to redouble their efforts to make sure that the reorganization and re-resourcing changes were going to be completed on time. You will also have to organize a meeting of your company's Board of Directors and shareholders. It is time to formally form the board.

I arrived an hour before the staff meeting with even more good news. Two more had accepted seats on the board. That gave us a full complement for the first meeting.

Getting Ready

The staff meeting was a complete success. The whole team had been working very hard to prepare for standing up the board. They had come face to face with major difficulties and overcame them.

It was clear that the reorganization and re-resourcing work could be completed within the next month. I could see a great deal of pride reflected in their eyes. And in truth, they had every right to be proud. They had substantially reinvented your company in an amazingly short period of time. It had developed from the proverbial ninety pound weakling to a well-muscled athlete that was eager for the next challenge.

We had added three very senior individuals to the team. The money spent on middle-level business development types had been reduced while additional people had been brought in to beef up proposal development and capture. We had also organized a standing pool of very senior individuals for the red teams and a virtual network of experts to be called upon on an as needed basis. It was clear that your company will be ready to meet its new advisory board within the next sixty days.

A new Chief Administrative Officer (CAO) had been in place for a couple of months and was taking large chunks of work off of your desk. Her remit included finance, human resources and quality control. Lots of senior time was being freed up.

About halfway through the staff meeting the focus shifted to preparing to work with individual board members. Two broad areas needed attention. The materials that would be provided to members for their use in their role as advocates for the company needed to be finalized up. Also plans had to be developed for working with individual members to target their first piece of business.

We meet over lunch. "Well, the pace is certainly picking up. I can feel my guys' energy levels going up – and my adrenaline is certainly working overtime. And, by the way, I'm starting to really appreciate the wisdom of clearing my schedule and those of my senior team. When you first told me that I would need to clear half my time for working with the board I thought that you are exaggerating. But after this morning's session I think you may have been too conservative."

Wait until the afternoon session. Once we start planning for working with individual board members targeting specific pieces of business the pace is going to pick up even more. And wait until you finally start to do business with the board. They are a fast crowd. You and your team have been in training for this and I think you're ready for it. But don't be surprised if your team has trouble keeping up.

After lunch the team breaks into working groups with each focusing on a specific board member. They generate modified materials for use in approaching specific types of clients. But before we broke you make a comment that sets the tone for the afternoon sessions. "I've already had calls from two of the board members. They wanted to let me know how pleased they were to be on our advisory board. They also began to sketch out specific pieces of business that they wanted to pursue. We've got a tiger by the tail here and we better be as good as they expect us to be. Actually we've got five tigers and we need to be quick as well as very good."

Meeting the Press

There were other activities that needed attention. The PR firm got out a press release. They had been briefed on the advisory board and alerted that an announcement was imminent. We had already reviewed a draft release. Now we have the names to fill in the blanks. Your company is about to get a heavy dose of positive branding!

It was also time for you to get out before the media. With a spade work done, we were ready for interviews and radio and television appearances. The PR firm has organized a campaign complete with media targets and collateral materials. We arranged for board members to provide quotes for the press release. In one case a new member is interviewed by local media. The buzz is on and every employee of your company seems to be aware that something very good was happening.

Off to Sea

In this case we put the first board meeting on one of my very favorite venues – a three-day cruise to the Bahamas. Initially you that receive this suggestion skeptically. *"That seems to me a bit of a boondoggle,"* you observe. But I explained that a cruise is an ideal venue - it is a controlled environment - in a way that no land based event is. I also explained that it is cost effective, more conducive to developing strong personal relationships and that the facilities on the particular ships that we select were head and shoulders above those that most land based resorts offer.

I show you that the cruise will cost about 60% of the land-based options. That is enough to close the deal. So a cruise to the Bahamas it is.

The time between the staff meeting and departure for the board meeting is high pressure for the team. They implement the last bits of the strategic plan. They also finish work on the materials that the members would be using. We organize a teleconference to brief the new board members and provide them with a detailed agenda, information on the venue and metrics for measuring success of the meeting.

Two weeks prior to departure each board member receives a detailed package which includes both the generic and focused material. They also receive a full set of travel documents – including information on the ship, itinerary, ports of call and shore excursions.

Four days before departure we have a staff meeting to review the agenda, objectives, metrics and assignments. Everything and everybody is ready – time to take it to sea!

Departure Day

There's something about arriving at the port and seeing the huge cruise liner that is going to be your home for the next few days. And there's something transformational that occurs when you cross that gangplank onto the ship. It is like the first steps on a journey to another world; definitely taking you outside the box and generating a feeling of expanding horizons and possibilities. No matter how many times I do it, I get the same rush.

The group assembles on the pool deck. They began arriving as soon as the ship opened for check-in. Most still have their 'land faces' on but I know that will quickly pass. By the time they have a couple of drinks and a bit of steel drum music the relaxed environment begins to work its magic.

We were a substantial clan. By the look on your face I can see that your are realizing that a very potent group was assembling. All of the board members and most of your senior team have come with traveling companions. There is an air of excitement and anticipation and a flurry of toasts to the future of the company and the board.

By the time the group settled down to the first dinner I can see the beginnings of a real camaraderie emerging. Like Nero Wolfe, I have a rule about dinner – *"no business is discussed"*. Like Rex Stout's great fictional detective, I think that humans ought to talk about other things occasionally. So that first dinner is a social occasion; with people getting to know each other. Another of my rules came in handy; *"you can't sit next to your traveling companion at dinner"*. It always amazes me how much more active table conversation is as a result. So everybody complies. It is a wonderful experience – seeing a board come to life before my eyes.

Day One – At Sea

"Ladies and gentlemen, let's come to order. Some of us have a full schedule of work before us and a full day tomorrow as well. Others are eager to get to the pool."

That's how the day starts. I call the board into existence.

During my initial remarks, I reviewed the schedule and objectives and described the non-business parts of the itinerary. There are shore excursions to consider and we had arranged a meeting in Nassau with some local business people. I also brief the group on the ship, dining arrangements and provided informational packets to all. After that the traveling companions headed to the pool deck and the rest of us settled down to business.

The morning is dedicated to presentations by the Chief Operating Officer and Senior Vice President of Business Development. Both are tasked to deliver a summary of the preparations that have been undertaken and to review important materials. First up was the COO.

I never coach executives in these kinds of situations. My philosophy is that, aside from making sure that they don't hit the nuclear button, mistakes are a constructive part of learning. Let me tell you about one COO who made one right off. He came prepared with a forty-slide deck and proceeded to plow through it as if he is briefing a bunch of middle level managers. I think he got to slide number five before one of the board members shut him down.

"Look, we already know most of this stuff and don't need you reading these slides to us. As I see it there are some basic things that we need to know. Let's focus on them."

The rest of the board members nodded in agreement. Fifteen minutes later the COO has a new agenda and an unused deck of slides. Here is the core of what the members are getting at:

"We can get you in the door and act as advocates for the company. But how are you going to make us comfortable taking that risk? How can we be sure that you won't mess up and loose the business - and damage our reputations to boot?"

By the end of that two-hour session it is clear to the team that the learning curve is going to be much steeper than they had anticipated. Board members are aggressively testing them and their preparations. The company is being held to a new and much higher set of standards. The board members are speaking in very clear and forceful terms.

To their credit, the team responded well. Where they had no answers they admitted it. They are clearly back on their heels. During the half-hour coffee break I met with them. The COO said, *"Wow, these old guys sure can set a fast pace. They don't mess around with pleasantries either. And they really seem to know what they are doing. I've never been through so much in such a short time."*

My reply was direct. "You are getting a real time education in the way very successful people approach things. There is, as my Scottish ancestors would say, 'nae daffin tolerated here'. You did well to pick up the pace. Remember, most of these people have built and managed organizations much larger and more successful than your company. They are a fast crowd. Learn from them when something like this happens. Take their lead – they know what they are talking about. Take their concerns seriously. Engage with them as mentors that have already decided that you and your company are worth the effort. Remember, you are still on probation. Prove yourselves worthy of their trust!"

The next session involved a presentation by the Senior Vice President of Business Development. In an attempt to simplify things he threw out the original slide deck and reduced things to a single slide. This is what it looked like:

Working with Board Members
        1)   you get us in
   2)   we establish credibility

3) we respond to the need
4) we get the business

He got as far as the second point when one of the Board Members jumped in with *"when I get you into a meeting you'll have all the credibility you need to close the deal – you don't build credibility – you need to avoid losing it!"*

The resulting discussion focused sharply on the fact that each board member was determined that their association with the company not damage their reputation in any way – that it would only enhance it.

The discussion moved on to a reprise of the work that had been done in preparation of the board's launch. This is the first time members see the true breadth of the board's potential. It is also the first time they see evidence of the dedication of other board members.

The CEO presented the afternoon session. The remit was to focus on important company quals, to introduce the new materials and to outline the basis for working with the board members. Early in the session the issue of the value of a certification came up. The company received one that is prominently displayed on all its literature. A member asked "what is the value of this certification to me as a client – other than making you more expensive and taking you longer to deliver?"

The resulting discussion demonstrated a blind-spot that many companies have. It is very good at justifying the value to other people who have bought into the certification regime. But these guys were asking from the perspective of a potential client. Preaching to the choir had no impact here. The question was *"what was the addition of the certification to the value proposition from the client's perspective."* As the session breaks up it is clear that the senior team needed to develop an answer.

Later that night I come across the entire team. They had claimed a section of one of the many lounges on the ship and are earnestly working the problem that the afternoon session has presented. The COO summarized the group's focus. "We have always taken as a given that the certification is seen as a good thing but we never looked at it from the perspective of a client. The board is forcing us to do that because they know it will be a major question in the minds of people they introduce us to. I'm convinced that it does add to the value proposition but we need to be able to communicate that effectively. We also need to realize that this has been, and will continue to be, a major concern in the minds of every potential client."

The CEO added, "I used to tell people that one of my strong points was that I looked at the world through the eyes of our clients. But the board has put us all to shame. They have the vision we need to gain."

Experiences like those described above are very common in initial board meetings.

Day Two – Nassau

The morning of the second day finds the ship in the beautiful harbor of Nassau. We are going to spend a whole day there. The traveling companions have already chosen shore excursions or decided on a day of shopping. But for the team and the board it is a day of work – with maybe a little time for play later on.

The schedule involves a morning series of breakout groups with individual board members to discuss specific pieces of business. The task is to come up with a detailed plan for targeting, proposal development, approach, delivery and capture. The resulting plans will be submitted to the whole group during an afternoon session.

During the afternoon session each board member takes the lead in presenting their plan. Key members of your team supports them. During each presentation other members will chime in with observations or offers of support through their own contacts. I can see that the mix was really starting to work.

My job is to monitor the presentations and keep an eye out for indications of weaknesses. I see one member who seems to be less aggressive than the others. Most might not have caught it but it did stands out to me and I made a mental note to have a one-on-one conversation. But for the most part things go extremely well. By the time the group breaks up and headed for Nassau we have detailed plans for approaching five major pieces of new business. I noticed that your feet did not seem to be touching the ground and the smile on your face is yards wide. Your company has a working advisory board.

Day Three – Journey to a Private Island

Day three is given over to socializing. The itinerary was chosen to allow a more social schedule if the work during the prior two days had came out OK. Morning finds the ship at the cruise line's private island. It's time to play.

During my initial remarks I had suggested a volleyball tournament between the board and the management team. That suggestion was taken up so, with the help of the cruise director, one was organized. The board wins – giving credence to Waylon Jennings' observation that 'old age and treachery always overcomes youth and skill.' It is a great time and everybody is celebrating the work that they have done.

Lunch is in a private setting. I notice that the two groups have merged. The early tendency to sit apart from each other is gone. There is also an air of celebration – lots of toasts to the future and reflections on how far they had come in such a short time.

Day Four – Return to Port

The group that disembarks is very different form the one that gathered on the pool deck just three days earlier. There are real friendships developing. Board members have come to know and respect your team. They are even more committed to helping your company grow. You and your team have begun to realize the true depth and breadth of the resource that they had access to.

You and I shared a flight home. "*I never thought a cruise could be so productive or so packed with important things that needed doing. When you first suggested it I was afraid it was going to be a leisurely journey with little getting accomplished. This was a very busy time – with lots going on and much accomplished. The foundations are laid for a very productive working relationship with the board. I am excited at the possibilities.*"

I have seen a few things slightly differently. But that was to be expected. My job was to take the long view and anticipate challenges before they came into full flower. There were stresses that needed tending to. One board member looked to me like he was going to be a problem. And your team needs a bit of attention. But, for the flight, I let you bask in the glow of a rising sun.

Change Management

Let's take a break from the narrative to talk a bit about some of the terms I've been using. The principal components of change management as used here involve:

o   professionalization of a corporate culture,
o   restructuring and re-resourcing of an organization, and
o   a restructuring and augmentation of a management team

An over-arching issue is the implementation and monitoring of the change plan. These are very complex and subtle processes. They must be closely coordinated. To go back to a previous example, it is like deciding to put a new, more powerful engine in an old car frame. You must prepare the frame for the forces that it will experience with the new power plant. The board is the engine while all the rest is the frame – context must be as well managed as the object.

There are significant downsides of poor coordination and implementation. The biggest ones can be grouped under the heading of negative branding. Building and standing up an advisory board is a high-profile undertaking. If you screw it up, lots of important people will know! Additionally you could end up wasting precious resources and dissipating the enthusiasm and momentum that brought the company to the point where it can benefit from an advisory board.

Because the risks are so high, management change is the major challenge to a management team looking to stand up an advisory board.

Professionalizing the Corporate Culture

Professionalization describes a process which is part science and part art. In this context, it describes the evolution of a corporate culture from talented armature status to that of experienced and proven pro. Think of it this way:

Jack Harris was a talented quarterback for Nowhere State. He led his team to a state championship three times during his college career and in his final season they were undefeated. The take on Jack was that he could pick a defense apart.
So the draft comes and Jack gets picked early on. When he shows up to training camp for his first pro season, he is full of himself and confident that he will quickly assume a leadership role on the team. But experience quickly disabuses him of that expectation. Jack comes face to face with a widely known fact. In football offensive players generally mature during college but defensive players take a bit more time to come into their prime. Jack was playing with amateurs. Now he is playing with pros. The defense is just better. They are picking apart his offence. What Jack got away with in college just doesn't work with the pros. He is going to have to lift his game substantially to even just survive.

The same is true with corporate cultures. When an advisory board is put in place there are two sets of pros that enter the field. The first are the board members. These are very experienced pros towards the ends of their careers. They know how the game is played and what it takes to win. Members also tend to be very good judges of human potential – and how well individuals are living up to their potential. For the most part, they are quick, decisive and unerringly right. They are a group that can unnerve a quarterback!

The second set of pros is the higher-up decision makers that the company will be put in contact with by board members. They will not be presenting to the 'flack catchers' anymore.

Here is an example of what I mean. I built a board for a company that did a lot of business with the Navy. The senior team was used to making extended initial presentations to junior officers – presentations that often did not generate any subsequent business. That was before the board was put in place.

One of their new board members was a retired senior flag officer. He made arrangements with a couple fellow admirals to introduce the company to the 'E' ring of the pentagon. "You are going to have fifteen minutes." Was the way he described the scheduled meetings. "You've only got two weeks to prepare for it. You better get cracking."

After his message sank in, we went to work with the senior team. They distilled their value proposition and quals down to the point that they could be delivered well within the time frame and still allow for Q&A. Their presentation focused on the business that they wanted to bid on and connected the value proposition and quals directly to the client's needs.

We practiced delivery over and over and brought in members of the red-team to role play the admirals. The result was that they could deliver a high-powered message in a very short time – no nonsense, no irrelevancies and *nae daffin*!

The point is that the standards and expectations of these senior people are going to be substantially higher than the company is used to meeting – and their fuse is going to be much shorter in the face of people who just don't seem to understand who they are talking to and what the situation demands. It is no place for amateur behaviors. Many times the team needs to draft some experienced players and help their stars move up just to deliver what is expected. In the end they need to be seen as understanding what is necessary and doing what is necessary to deliver it.

As a culture professionalizes, there are behaviors which simply won't work in this brave, new world. Much of what passed for management during the village stage will prove inadequate. Reporting patterns, fuzzy overlapping of authority and responsibility and back passages to top management will have to be re-examined and most replaced. The garage-stage tendencies, like the toys of childhood, will have to be left behind as the company matures.

The best way to kick a professionalization into high gear is to bring in senior types with lots of experience and knowledge. These 'grains of sand' can serve as the stimulus for the pearls. As mentors they can add a whole new dimension to the corporate culture in a relatively short time.

Restructuring and Re-resourcing the Organization

I often describe this process as re-dreaming the company. It involves seeing the company in a new way. Often I suggest that the senior team do a bit of reading about complexity theory as an antidote for the post-Fordist perspectives that have most often dominated their thinking. The suggestion that it is productive to look at a company as a complex self-organizing entity – a living organism with its own needs, tendencies and appetites - is often seen as a radical idea at first. But I highly recommend the perspective – particularly during efforts at accelerated growth.

Capabilities and enthusiasms which sustained and drove forward a company in its early years will no longer be sufficient. Like a growing child, the company's needs change – the list of resources that are critical change – the drives evolve – the institutional knowledge has to expand.

One of the major requirements in this area is the redefinition of roles, authority, responsibilities and prerogatives. It's not just that new job descriptions need to be evolved and implemented (they surely do) but the new structure has to serve the needs of a growing company – one that is moving from adolescence to adulthood! The organism is growing up.

As it grows its needs evolve. As resources are integrated into its mix, the balance of resources at its disposal also needs to change. This is particularly true when you add an advisory board to the mix. Here are a couple of examples:

The business development team will almost certainly need a major overhaul. Most companies use middle-level executives in the front-line hunt for new business. With a board in place, there needs to be a decreased emphasis on the middle level business development types. At the same time the resourcing of proposal development and capture areas will have to be expanded substantially.

As a prelude to bringing a board online, the corporate infrastructure almost always needs to be beefed up. Two areas which ordinarily need the most work are human resources and financial control and reporting.

Human resources will come under increased pressure on a number of fronts. They will have to deal with much more substantial increases in the workforce over a much shorter time horizon. In some cases they will be asked to deal with an entirely new requirement – the need to have people 'on the beach' – ready for deployment. As the organization grows quickly the knowledge, systems and experience needed to manage HR will increase. Unfortunately as organizations grow the possibility of lawsuits grows as well. HR is often one of the most poorly managed sources of corporate liability.

Financial control and reporting will often be in much the same situation. It is not just a matter of putting more sophisticated and robust reporting systems in place. The company will need a more complex approach to arranging for and managing financial resources. The need for Financial Vice President-level skills will become more acute. The CEO and COO will find less and less time to spend on these matters but will have a more acutely felt need to be informed about them.

Both of these areas need to be professionalized. After all, you don't just upgrade the steering wheel – you need to do the same for the shock absorbers and breaks!

Management team restructuring and augmentation is always a major part of the preparation for standing up an advisory board. The first step is an assessment of the strengths and weaknesses of the current team – not in terms of the current levels of business but the rapid growth that is being planned. The assessment is designed to identify those team members who will be able to grow along with the company as well as those who are probably not going to be able to make the journey.

Most organizations have these two types of employees in senior positions. Senior management needs to sort out both. I recommend an employee and team assessment as an initial step. These represent an inexpensive way to get a handle not only on the current capabilities of your people but their interest, potential and capability to grow. Once they are identified a company needs to implement an aggressive program dedicated to the education and training of these key team members.

It is hard to overstate the impact that adding sure hands trained through extensive experience in larger organizations can have on a company. People who are experienced with professional systems and approaches can bring with them knowledge and judgment that will help a company navigate the difficult process of accelerating growth. They will help the company up its game and play at the level necessary. They will also bring additional of skill sets that are necessary to manage a rapidly growing organization. The balance between this 'new blood' and 'developing indigenous talent' is a major challenge.

As the team grows it is vitally important to deploy an integration strategy which will insure that cliques do not form – schisms within the team. Apart for the obvious reasons there is one that merits special mentioning. These very experienced people will tend to act as mentors to others. That can seem a threat to the position of other members of the senior team – the CEO in particular. But these mentoring relationships will be a key factor in the ability of the company to manage the change needed to prepare for the board. You have to let them happen.

The change management plan needs to be a formal and holistic document – a reference that all parties can use to measure progress. It is important that it manages a seamless integration of the strategic and tactical. It also should contain very specific metrics for each component. The latter is very important because there will be conflicts over performance and implementation – tensions which will arise because of divergent agendas. There will be a lot of pressure. A well-structured and presented strategic plan will go a long way to easing these strains.

The implementation of the plan should be assigned to a team that draws from across the entire company – not just the senior levels. This committee should have regular review meetings and be able to engage in frank and direct conversations – it should not finesse any issue no matter how minor it seems. It should also be tasked to make sure that the burdens do not fall onto the shoulders of one or two team members – a very common occurrence in these situations.

Conflict, Renegotiation and Removal

"We have a problem on the board that you and I need to sort out." It always happens and the conversation generally begins with me delivering that message.

The Need to Act

That is how our meeting began some six months plus after the board's launch. I had been monitoring the members during that time and it was becoming clear that we were going to have problems with one of them.

That is not to say that there hadn't been other bumps along the way. An advisory board focused on driving the run rate is a complex organization made up of complex parts. There were stresses as pressures to deliver results increased. Sometimes, those pressures surfaced in non-productive ways. Your team occasionally stumbled and needed to be brought back into line. But the board members were getting good at that and the team was responding well.

This was a different kind of problem altogether. This member just wasn't working out. He seemed fascinated by conversations about management and was often second guessing the CEO. He was increasingly unresponsive to management's requests for reports. He also had a high opinion of himself and his position in the world. But that wasn't converting into progress towards getting business. Now, he was beginning to disrupt the rest of the board and negatively brand the effort. So you and I sit down to review options. This is how it went:

I think that we're going to have to replace Dave. I see three areas where he is coming up short. First, despite my conversations with him, he continues to be convinced that his reputation is so strong that all he has to do is make introductions and the business belongs to the company. It is very difficult to get him to follow up or stay with the team as they pursue leads. He also continues to insist that introductions rather than advocacy are his appropriate contributions. His overblown sense of self-importance is clearly not subscribed to by those who he is introducing us to. His initiatives are not progressing. The value is not there for us.

As you know, I have just applied the metrics that we agreed to as a result of our six-month review of board performance. I have reviewed the results of all members. Dave is the only one that did not measure up. When I reviewed these findings with him he became argumentative then defensive. He will probably not take the metrics seriously and will continue to phone it in.

Second, Dave is not adding to the board meetings. As other members' efforts move us closer to actually capturing business, he has become more and more dismissive of them and their efforts. He seems to want to have the same conversations over and over again - probably to avoid admitting that he is failing in his obligations to the company and the rest of the board. This is having a corrosive effect. I have had a couple of other members mention this. It isn't lethal to the board but it does potentially limit its effectiveness.

Finally, I got a call from a friend who asked me specifically about him. It seems that Dave has been talking out of school on us. Dave ran into him at a bar and he got an ear full. Our board member explained how neither you nor I really understood how the world worked and that the board was not going to work out. In addition to a failure of morality, this amounts to negative branding and we need to deal with it right away.

Despite our careful selection process and subsequent efforts to maintain a clear understanding with all board members, this one is heading south. I recommend that we replace Dave. If you agree, I request that you write a letter asking Longview to terminate Dave's board membership. If you do concur, we should move quickly.

You take a bit of time to reflect on my recommendations. "OK, the team has also had conversations about Dave and his lack of significant contribution. The truth is that he has become a sort of caricature of the 'bad member'. I think they are losing respect for him. The last board meeting put the difference between Dave and the rest of the members into high relief. I agree – it's time to make a move. Let's do it. I'll dictate the letter right away. How do we proceed from here?

It's pretty simple – not nearly as complicated as removing a sitting director. The agreement that we have says that Dave can be removed without cause at any time. He can also leave the board without explanation at any time. I will meet with Dave and let him know that the company has decided to terminate his membership on the board.
Will we have any legal exposure as a result of the termination?

No significant exposure. It will be important that neither you nor any member of your team engage in any conversations – public or private - about the termination – positive or negative. Dave will be asked to do the same. We will issue a neutral statement as part of the announcement of his successor stating that Dave has left the board. I will let him know about my conversation – as we have some indication that he is talking out of school – and will ask him to cease. I will also make it clear that, if any of the initiatives that he has started pay off, he will be compensated according to the. And that should be that.

I had a cup of coffee while you draft the letter and passed it by the corporate council. The lawyer brought in the letter for his signature and we discussed the marching orders for me and the team. I also reviewed the conversation that I was going to have with Dave. The next step was a meeting with Dave – one I was not looking forward to. But it was my job.

Prior to actually meeting with Dave I called each of the other board members and briefed them confidentially on the decision. None of them were surprised at the turn of events. It always amazes me how much ownership most board members quickly come to have in the board they are on and how much concern they evidence for the welfare of the company.

Meeting with a Departing Member

I called Dave and suggested a meeting. At first he was resistive. I am sure that he suspected. But I was insistent and we decided to meet the next day.

Dave, the company has decided to ask you to step down from its advisory board.
I wasn't sure what the look on Dave's face was meant to communicate. On the one hand it looked a bit relieved while on the other there seemed to be surprise.

Might I ask why?

As you know, we have completed a performance review of all board members using the metrics that we all agreed to at the very beginning. I discussed the results of that review with you by telephone last week. Yesterday I delivered the findings to the company. Their decision was to ask you to resign from the board.
And what if I won't?

Then they will remove you under the terms of your agreement. Either way you will be off the board. They just wanted to give you a chance to take the initiative.
What about the things that I have going?

The company will stand by its obligation to pay you in the event that business is actually gained according to the terms of its agreement with you. Further, the company will issue a statement indicating that you have left the board without any comment on the circumstances. It will be made simultaneously with the announcement of your replacement.

I would appreciate them not making a big thing about it.

You can count on that. Additionally, the management team will be under orders not to comment on your departure in any way. I don't expect that they will be asked – but the bases will be covered. There is one thing that I need to mention. A good friend of mine told me that you had a conversation with him in which you disparaged me, the board and the company. I'm not interested in debating what you said. I am only making the point that the company is prepared to agree that this just didn't work out and part company. But, if they find out that these kinds of conversations are taking place, they will get very aggressive. Have I made myself clear?

Yes you have and I appreciate the directness. I did have the conversation and regretted it almost immediately. I will let him know that he should forget what I said because it is not true and I really didn't mean it. I guess I felt over my head on the board and ego got the best of me. Tell the team and board members that I apologize.

I'll do that. Here is the agreement to withdraw. Take a read and, if it is OK, sign a copy for me. Your withdrawal from the board will be effective immediately.

Dave read the agreement and signed a copy. "I'm sorry that this didn't work out. Maybe next time."

Dave paid the check and left me to enjoy the rest of my cigar. I never like these meetings but they occur regularly enough when you are dealing with something as complex as advisory boards. I headed back home knowing that the next meeting at the company's office was likely to be a far happier one. The board was getting ready to draw first blood!

First Blood

The first 'big win' is always an emotional one for the management team and the board. It is a solid indication that what they have invested so much time and energy into is starting to pay off. This morning's teleconference was focused on what looked to be the first big piece of business that the board had generated. It had been in existence for a little more than nine months. They were getting close on a number of chunks of business but one was particularly sweet. And it looked to come in first.

The company had a longstanding relationship with one particular client. They had had a number of contracts that extended over multiple years and were highly rated by the client as a valued provider. This good relationship had allowed them to gradually increase their business base. Several employees had offices within the client's facilities and there was a fairly constant dialogue about other challenges that the company might help with. The company/client relationship was close and very positive.

One board member had a very positive impact on this already strong relationship. He had a strong reputation in the space that the client served. He also had a number of professional relationships with senior executives of the client. Finally, he had a strong knowledge of the space and was seen as a visionary by many in it. His decision to hitch his wagon to the company was widely seen as an endorsement of the company and its management team; it began to be known as his guys!

Shortly after joining the board he commenced a series of meetings that involved not only the senior team from the client but experts in the field. You supported the formation of this group and the company served as its informal sponsor.

The group came to be seen as one where quality thinking about the future was done – and the company benefited by being its sponsor.

On one evening, the board member was having drinks with the CEO of the client. She wanted to thank him for putting together the 'thinking group' and for the benefits that her company was realizing from it. They had been able to identify a new direction – another market application for one of their products. It was a major opportunity and she was grateful.
"I need to thank you for the work you did in putting together the. We have identified a major opportunity because of our participation in it – one that none of our competitors seem to have picked up on. We owe you big time. Thanks."

"Happy to be of help. Truth is that I've enjoyed pulling the group together. It has really stretched me out and got me thinking about new approaches to old problems. I can't remember when I've been so mentally sharp. It's like being back at MIT."

"Before we get misty-eyed about college days, I've got something I'd like to talk to you about. I know that you've been helping the company. They seem to have come a long way in a short time. There is sharpness about them that wasn't there before. I suspect that you and the other board members have had something to do with that. Some of the work they have been doing for us is considerably above their usually high standard.

We recently received a proposal from them on an extension of work they are doing for us. It was a sharply focused and professional piece of work. They touched all of the bases and hit the ball out of the park. We like the company and look forward to doing business with them – but this was a real bonus."

157

"The board has been running them pretty hard. Dr. Smith has been managing a red-teaming process that is at the pro level. But more importantly the team is really upping its game. It seems like every employee is determined not to let the company or the team down. Board members have taken note. After an early rough patch the team has risen to the occasion. The company has also brought in some world-class talent. They have a virtual network of resources that is very impressive.

I'll be honest with you. When I first went on the board I had one eye on the door. They were asking me to be a strong advocate – not just provide introductions – and put in a lot of effort to help them up their game. This approach to advisory boards was very new to me. Dr. Smith put us in a real working harness and starting cracking the whip. Recently he removed one of the members for 'non-production.' These guys are not playing around. The board is having a huge impact on the company."

"I've heard that he is pretty good at cracking the whip. I'm not sure that I would have put up with it."

"Well, if you have the chance, give it a try. You may get to the point where you want to get into what I am sure the Chief would call your 'grandmotherly mode'. I'll tell you one thing, is a lot better than sitting on a bunch of mind-deadening boards. I wouldn't trade the experience for a dozen seats on ordinary ones. But you had something you wanted to discuss."

"Yes I do. We have a piece of business that is much larger than what we normally put out to the company. It is about a hundred million dollars over five years. In the past we would not have taken them seriously on something like this but now we are prepared to. But, before I let the proverbial gene out of the bottle, I wanted to get your recommendation. I know that you have a fiduciary relationship with the company and I don't want you to violate that."

"Actually, that's not strictly true Mary. As a member of their advisory board I am bound to help them find and capture new business. But I don't have the same relationship with the company as their directors do. If I don't think they are up to what you have in mind, I'll tell you."

"Thanks – that will help al lot. Anyway, this business is central to our value proposition and we would be betting a big chunk on the company and its team. I'd like to walk you through it and get your reaction to the possibility that they would be invited to bid."

She did exactly that. She outlined in detail the work required and it's important to her company. As friends, they were able to have a frank and open discussion of the possibilities. He was able to analyze the company's strengths and weakness – and to assure her that the weaknesses would be addressed by the CEO and his team with close monitoring by me and the board. In the end, she decided to allow him to carry the news to the CEO – they were invited to bid on the business.

As soon as she left, he was on the phone to the CEO. "You need to get over here right away. I have something you are going to enjoy hearing!"

That was enough to get the CEO's attention. He walked the ten minutes from the offices to the bar in anticipation. He knew that the member was well a serious player on the board. As cryptic as his call way, the CEO knew that good things were afoot.

"OK, what's up? You look like the proverbial cat that just

swallowed the canary!"

"You might way that. I just had a session with a friend. She wanted my opinion on something and I was more than pleased to give it to her."

He reviewed his conversation and could see the CEO's eyes getting bigger as he talked. After a detailed description of the weakness of the company's team that would have to be addressed, the board member got to the punch line. "It's yours to bid on. Just make sure that you don't screw it up."

The rest of the evening was spent roughing out an action plan that included proposal development, red-teaming and presentation. The also developed a plan for dealing with her concerns – identifying changes that would have to be made in order to get the company in a dominate position to win the business.

That evening was the first step in a process that resulted in the company submitting what was sure to be a life altering proposal. In the end they beat out their competition and the scuttlebutt was that they were about to win the business.

Two of her concerns merit mentioning here. The first one dealt with the company's ability to ramp up its workforce fast enough to deliver under the contract. The HR department had responded with an aggressive but plausible plan that had been a central part of the proposal and a big factor in their win. She was also concerned that the company might not have the internal resources to adequately supervise the work. The team put together an oversight plan that drew on key resources in the company's virtual network.

The business was won and the run-rate of the company was increased by forty percent overnight. The board had made its mark – they were on the in the game.

Managing The Board

Board meetings are the middle parts of a process which fills the entire calendar year. A company needs to recognize this in order to adequately manage it. In this section I want to talk a bit about the preparation for, management and follow up of the actual meetings. Next I will spend some time on the management of the board between meetings. Finally I will discuss the metrics that are most useful in measuring the progress and contributions of the board.

Rule Number One

The first rule of managing advisory boards as business development engines is to cultivate the emergence and deepening of purposefulness. By that I mean seeing that the culture of the board is focused on obtaining results through the combined, purposeful actions of the members and the company's management team.

As its top priority, management needs to help the board members become engaged in the future of the company. Initially most board members will be eager to engage but still not integrated into the culture of the company. The board will, at first, be seen as an add-on that the senior team has organized. Both of these situations need to be changed quickly.

Board members need to become 'part of the family'. It is important that they feel very deeply connected with the company and its employees. When this happens, they will feel welcomed by the employees and free to communicate with them in a productive and creative way. Management needs to allow this to happen. Any attempts to keep the board as the 'private preserve' of the senior team will limit the board's effectiveness.

Employees need to see the board as a valuable addition to the company's ability to grow. They have to get to know about the members, their backgrounds, experience and range of contacts as well as their commitment to the company. This is a particularly challenging process as a certain level of formality needs to be maintained. You don't want employees to engage in a lot of ancillary communications with members but you do need to have them supplying important information that will increase the chances of winning new business. Professional courtesy needs to be maintained – particularly with very busy and highly experienced individuals.

Management needs to put in place a program focused first on educating employees about the board – its purpose, function and role. Employees need to know what intelligence to gather and how to pass it up the line. These reporting systems should not be overly engineered. For the most part, I generally recommend that a central clearing point for each member be established within the senior team.

Management should consider a compensation scheme for employees who gather and pass on important information. Even small rewards such as certificates of recognition are important. For big 'gets' that result in new business gained, cash or options are often a good idea. Incentives should be focused on the provision of meaningful and actionable intelligence.

Remember, purposefulness is the Holy Grail – purposefulness that extends from the senior team through the board – purposefulness that extends down through the ranks. Peak board impact requires a holistic approach to these two challenges.

One area that I focus on as the board stands up is the evolution of the relationships between the board members and the senior team – particularly the CEO. For most CEOs, dealing with the kind of experienced talent that tends to be assembled can be a challenge to their self-confidence. Behaviors can range from the deferential to avoidance of taking command. Some CEOs simply don't provide the necessary leadership. Others try to micro manage the board. There is a delicate balance that needs to be reached. One of the reasons that I stay involved with the board and its management is to help members of the senior team attain this balance.

Early on, I work with the team to help them see the real dynamics that are possible. Members are eager to get to work – to help the company grow. They are going to look to the team for leadership and structure.

"These five people have more total experience than the whole of my senior team. Every one of them has met and mastered challenges that I am still struggling with. How can I presume to lead them? Where do I get off telling Mt. Rushmore to follow me?"

That was how one CEO put it during a conversation we had just before the board was launched. I could see that he was realizing that soon the board would be formed and have its first meeting. *"How do I presume to lead?"*

During the early months of the board's operation, I was heavily engaged in facilitating the development of productive relationships. I worked closely with the CEO. It was a matter of getting him to realize that he had to put those self-doubts away and do the very best he could to provide leadership and structure for the members. He also had to make sure that his senior tem was on the same page. I organized a series of training and discussion events and, over the period of a couple of weeks, eased their concerns and got the team focused how they would productively participate with board members.

Early on this was one of the challenges that I tended to miss. But now it is one of the challenges that I focus attention on every time. Management cannot simply assume that they will be able to interact with the members. The board will not allow business as usual. Training in this area prior to launch is one of the most important contributors to a successful launch and purposeful board.

General Observations

A board both generates and lives on intelligence – in both senses of the word. Intelligent management assures that the board can live up to its potential. No matter how motivated and connected members are, poor management can dissipate enthusiasm and commitment very quickly. The primary burden for making a board work is on the management team of the company.

Synergy is a very important aspect of board performance. The gathering, processing and exchange of information are critical to magnifying its impact. Timely and highly useful information is the life blood of any board. Management can set the tone and standards for the gathering and dissemination of this information.

One of the biggest board-killers is the start-then-stop-then-start-then-stop mentality that can settle in if the management team thinks of the board only in terms of its meetings. A board needs to be managed year-round. Members should be engaged year-round. Each time a board stops makes it harder to start it up again. The process generates resistance and pressures. Imagine the cumulative effects of starting then stopping four times a year.

'Event relationships' with board members are the most negative possible outcomes of having a board. If your relationships are centered around the regular meetings and not truly year-round, members will begin to adopt the kind of behavior that I just described. These 'event relationships' become something akin to 'dating' rather than 'living together' and can be tentative in much the same sense. If you are looking to forge a solid lasting connection with these very influential people, you will need to deal with them on an ongoing rather than 'event' basis.

A board thrives on substance and dies when fed fluff. Management needs to make sure that substance is what the board receives. That means forget the 'press release' mentality and the 'chamber of commerce' fluff. You must deliver the kind of actionable intelligence and meaningful tasking that will result in real progress. Board members should not be contacted without purpose and should not be shown off as the 'stars' in the company's heavens. Remember this is a working board – both the management and board members should always have that front and center in their minds.

Board meetings, indeed every contact with any member, should be focused on action and results. Management should reach this understanding from the very beginning and be very careful of doing anything to dissipate it. Every meeting should have as its first agenda item a detailed review of progress towards capturing business that has been targeted. Every conversation about a particular piece of business should focus on winning it. Even discussions about new targets - 'brain-storming' discussions of the best ways to pursue these opportunities – should be done with purpose and focus. General discussions which do not conclude with action items and assignment of responsibility for follow-up are corrosive of board performance and should be avoided at all costs.

Remember that the best rule is to 'make heroes and avoid making scapegoats'! Meetings are very good venues in which to single out individuals that have made important contributions. By all means, public recognition is a good idea. It is important to keep that recognition in proportion to the contribution. Board members will realize when a pitch is being over-sold. That being said, other members will take note if the company pauses to recognize the contributions of one of its own.

On the other hand, poor performance should be dealt with privately. Most often these issues come up as a result of a member who is not producing. Many times direct conversations can correct the situation. I have seen members up their game as a result of being treated with consideration. And even if the process does not improve performance, private discussions will assure that the process of removing a member does not cause wider damage.

One question worth consideration is 'who chairs the meetings'? The logical choice might seem the CEO but there are good reasons for taking a more sophisticated view of the challenge. I suggest that the agenda be divided into segments and that leadership for each segment be assigned to the person most qualified to lead the discussion. Each time I have used this approach surprising things happen.

Schedule

The board should meet at least four times each year. The major meeting should be coordinated with the annual strategic planning review. Board member participation in this review can be very useful. It will assure that the plan takes into consideration important business opportunities. Involving the board will also strengthen the relationships with management and result in an increased 'buy-in' by members. A broader understanding of the company, its intended direction, resourcing needs and future will also be very useful.

I have seen these meetings productively run on for a couple of days – particularly when important issues such as a liquidity event, strategic partnership formation, major new initiative or significant management change are on the agenda. Sometimes issues will generate contention based on alternative views of the 'best way forward'. In these situations it is always a good idea to allow the process to run its course while the participants are face-to-face. In any case, I have always found it a good idea to allow extra time for this most important of all the board meetings.

One approach that I have found very useful is to schedule a presentation of the results of this meeting to either the board of directors or a committee of the outside directors. Both the management team and advisory board members participate in this presentation. The results can be truly galvanizing. Both the management and advisors are on the same page – and tied into the same strategic plan.

The meeting that takes place roughly six months after the major one should be focused on progress towards delivery on the strategic plan. It should also allow for a reconsideration of that plan where appropriate. I like to have this meeting face-to-face as well. Compatriots who go more than six months without sitting down and engaging tend to feel less connected.

The other two formally scheduled board meetings can be held via teleconference. These meeting must have the same levels of preparation, materials distribution and structure that the face-to-face one have. During all of these meetings the reinforcement of the purposefulness needs to be seen to – this is a working board about the serious business of growing the company.

The Materials

Here is a quick set of guidelines for preparing materials prior to a board meeting:
Completeness: Make sure that the package delivered to the members contains all relevant information that they well need to engage on the agenda items. I highly recommend that the package be delivered vie one e-mail or mailing. It is important not to put board members in the position of discussing issues that involve information or documents that they do not have in front of them. So make sure that they have all the materials that will be used during the meeting. In the event that there are last minute developments, make sure that they are transmitted in a high profile manner and verify that each member has received the update.

Timeliness: If at all possible, deliver the package, including the agenda, at least two weeks prior to the meeting. It is good form to contact each member a few days prior to the session in order to discuss any questions that have come up as a result of the package. This kind of preparation will focus the actual meeting on extending from the information provided rather than focusing on it. Remember that a productive meeting produces progress – from where it started to where it ended up. Timely provision of materials lays the ground for this kind of progress.

Professional presentations: This is particularly relevant when it comes to reports of a technical nature such as financials. These reports should use the professional standards in use by the company. If you ever have spent a frustrating couple of hours trying to reconcile poorly drawn actual performance reports with budget projections you'll know what I mean.

In usable form: Remember that some of the materials will be useful to members in their contact with potential clients. Get those documents into usable form prior to the meeting. If appropriate, consult with individual members prior to the session. Don't spend valuable meeting time revising documents!

Between Meetings

The meetings are just the pattern in the rug – there is the woof and warp – the context within which they take place – and that context is the key to broad productivity. Meetings should be a culmination of work done in the 'in-between' times and an opportunity for planning the next steps. The board needs to become a year-round operation. That means that the times between meetings should see the bulk of the activity. This is an important metric and an early indicator that something is going astray. A board that becomes active only in the run-up, during the meetings and the period shortly after will atrophy and turn non-productive.

Board members should be regularly updated on intelligence gathered. They should also be contributing information to the mix. *Ad hoc* sessions should be organized when new data indicates either a change in the status of an opportunity being pursued or a new opportunity that has been identified. In such an environment, board members can become valuable sources of high-level intelligence which, when combined with the more tactical information gathered by employees, can radically improve the results of business development efforts.

One particularly potent device is the creation of a special, limited access, virtual bulletin board for both the senior team and the members. It should be a place where new data can be posted with alerts automatically sent out. It should also give members an opportunity to post intelligence that will not be widely accessed.

Measuring the Results – Metrics

A board is a strategic investment that a company makes with a specific purpose in mind – increasing its growth rate. It should be treated just like any other strategic investment. The board should extend shareholder value by increasing the run-rate, adding to the status of the company in the eyes of potential clients and add to the value of the company in any liquidation event. As such, investment in a board is properly subjected to the same kind of cost/benefit analysis that other investment are.

What to Measure

The increase in the amount of business in the pipeline is the first metric that you need to pay attention to. This is a very easy metric to assess. Most companies keep data on their pipeline. The trend should become more sharply positive after the board's launch.

One early indicator of board vitality is the amount of time spent by board members in contact with potential clients. Whether in general or target conversations, board members should be engaged with important people that will help them identify potential new business. It is important that the senior contact with each member keep a log of conversations on this subject. Not only will these logs become important during meetings – they will also give an indication of the combined activity of the members on behalf of the company. These levels should deepen and widen over time.

Contact between the team and board members is another good indicator of the evolution of productive relationships. It is important that cumulative logs be kept of these contacts and that they are reviewed regularly by the CEO. You will want to look for patterns of both productive and unproductive contact. By reviewing these logs in executive session, a CEO can help his team improve their efforts to get the board operating effectively.

It is important to take the temperature of each member on a fairly regular basis. By that I mean finding out how the member is feeling about their involvement in the board, their role as an advocate for the company and their ability to make significant contributions to its growth. Focus on these issues can help a team identify important areas of work with specific members and support the development of action plans to overcome them.

It is important to remember that the time spent by the senior team is an investment in the board. Tracking senior team time should be part of the cost/benefit analysis. This approach will help focus team members on the productive contacts and reduce their tendency to engage in less productive communications. A system for tracking the time spend should be set up prior to launch of the board.

There are numerous services which track the buzz on a company. By buzz I mean the open source information – positive, negative or neutral – that flows through e-mails, chat rooms and other internet channels. I always recommend that a company arrange for tracking of the buzz. It is a very low cost way to find out how a company's reputation is evolving.

Keeping Track of the Pipeline

When dealing with assessing the pipeline, there are several factors that need to be taken into consideration. One is the leadership roles by members in identifying, targeting and capturing new business. Another is the volume and quality of the leads which each member generates. A third is the lead conversion into proposals. Finally there is the conversion of proposals into won business. Early on the first two factors will be measurable but an indication of the maturing of the board will be that all of these factors will come into play.

An important metric is the participation of the members beyond the initial, introduction stage. It is vitally important that they stay involved until either the business in won of the effort abandoned. This single indicator will separate out those members who have taken their obligations as advocates very seriously from those who see themselves as providing introductions. An effective member should play an important, ongoing role in any targeting and capture process which result from a lead generated.

Collateral Benefits

There are several collateral benefits that accrue to a company that has a board such as the one which I have been describing. Two are worth special mention. First, board members should be regularly bringing senior team members into contact with a wide range of important people. The range and depth of the networks of team members should increase over time. Second, members should be the source of new initiatives – particularly in the business development area. The company should be involved in 'pursuits' that they would not have if the board did not exist.

Reviewing Results

Two things are important about the review process. The first is that the data be provided to all parties – not just the conclusions. The second is that the review be conducted in a completely transparent way for all parties. These to approaches will turn performance review sessions into performance improvement sessions – and that is critical.

It is said that there are two kinds of approaches to managing poor performance. The first is to find someone to blame while the second is to find a way to fix the problem. It is the first behavior that has to be avoided. If reviews become the mechanism to improving performance they will b eagerly anticipated. Management – and the CEO in particular – needs to make this so.

Updating the Metrics

Every set of metrics should evolve with experience. Changes in metrics should be done with member collaboration and the changes should be ratified by consensus. Board members should be seen as a source of wisdom on this topic and their participation should be encouraged.

Anniversary

It has been a year since the launch of the board. We have been through a full series of meeting. But this meeting was to be different – it was going to be a strategic review/board meeting combined with an all-hands retreat.

It had been a very good year for your company. Two large pieces of business had been won and board members had been instrumental in helping to win them. One member had been replaced. The working relationships between the team and board members had survived some bumps but were now solid. The reputation of the board within the company had been established – they were a critical asset.

Everybody in the company had worked very hard to win and then deliver on the business. Both contracts were now underway. HR had responded magnificently. They had staffed up two engagements that together amounted to an eighty percent increase in the company's run-rate. Finance had put control systems in place in a highly professional manner. It was a joy to watch people do well what they wouldn't have thought themselves capable of doing at all ten months earlier. Everybody had pitched in and it was time to recognize that.

You decide that a symbolic return to where it all began was just the thing – back to sea and Nassau. So I organize the trip – including a chartered flight for the employees and their traveling companions. We put the group on the very same ship and the senior team and board members in the very same cabins that they had occupied a year before. It was going to be a very nostalgic journey for them.

There were several notable differences between the first and second planning review. The first trip had begun with many uncertainties and had concluded with many questions yet to be answered. The gathering on the pool deck was one of strangers getting to know each other. Some of the sessions were focused on negotiating the rules of engagement and establishing minimum conditions for involvement. Tensions came when the standards of the board members were stricter than those of the management team. It was a time or testing as well as one for deciding if the initial decisions were a good idea.

The return to Nassau was a different experience altogether. The board was obviously working and had proven itself as a very good investment. There were no strangers now – only friends who had fought and won battles or were engaged in battles that they expected to win. The rules of engagement had long ago been settled on and the management team had upped its game to meet a much higher set of standards. Now tensions came because of the need to win together. This was a time for celebrating and for looking forward into a future that was much more clearly defined.

It was also a time to recognize that the board's success had been possible only with the help of everybody within your company. All of the employees were invited and better than ninety percent of them attended. That amounted to about one hundred fifty employees and a like number of traveling companions. The group was over three hundred and fifty strong!

As a joke I prepared a comparison – how much more a land-based even would have cost the company – and attached a wry suggestion that the savings should be a bonus. You know that it is a joke – but two weeks after we returned a rather substantial check showed up. You didn't have to do it – but I remember the gesture and the recognition of the contribution that we had made to him and his company. It is experiences like that that make everything worthwhile.

175

The group that assembled on the pool deck was in a serious party mood. They knew that the company was on a path to increased success and they we ready to share the joy that they felt with their compatriots. The evening ended with a private karaoke session. To say 'a good time was had by all' would be an understatement.

We wisely allowed the group to sleep in that first morning at sea. We didn't see most of them until lunch. During the afternoon the employees participated in a series of meeting while the traveling companions enjoyed the ship.

During the first sessions the COO and SVP of business development made presentations. Both referred to their experiences the prior year. Their messages were strongly upbeat. Massive changes had occurred and the company was considerably more professional, better run and growing at an accelerated rate. The COO focused on a cost/ benefit analysis of the board. There was no question – the returns on the modest investment were paying off big time. After he finished, the business development team leader took that stage. Here presentation outlined the very substantial increase in the reach of the senior team and focused on the massive jump in positive buzz. I could tell that the audience was taking it all in and enjoying every minute of it.

Then you take the stage and introduce each of the board members. You take pains to provide information on the work that each had done and was doing. Each member also made short remarks. They are the stars of your presentation and your gratitude for their support and contributions to the future to the company is obvious to all. It was clear that they were comfortable being part of your team.

As the afternoon sessions came to a close, you take the stage again. This time you thanked the employees. They had responded magnificently. You singled out several for awards – for their efforts to gather intelligence and assist the board in identifying new business. With that done, you tell them that during the next two days they were 'off the clock'. *"Go and enjoy – the thing has been done well and you deserve a break."*

The business part of the trip was over for the employees but the senior team and board members still had work to do. The next morning we began the review of the strategic plan. One thing was different this time – the confidence levels were much higher. Much more seemed possible. The resulting update of the plan was a much more expansive vision for the company and a commitment from each participant to 'make it happen'.

I organize a special dinner in Nassau for the senior team and board members. The ground rules were specific – this is a session to frankly assess and learn from the successes, failures, challenges and advances that the board had experienced during the prior year. Over the years I have found this type of session very important in the maintenance and care of advisory boards.

The discussions were enabled by incredibly good food and lubricated with wonderful wine. Serious failures were frankly discussed without search for blame – only improvement. Successes were celebrated and sealed with toasts all around. Several recommendations were offered by members. The board should be expanded from five to seven with members added in two specific areas. Access to the private bulletin board should be expanded with a special 'reserve area' for very sensitive information. By the time that the cigars and brandy showed up, it was clear that this board had an identity that it was comfortable with and a management team that it had confidence in.

With business concluded, the senior team and board settled into a social mode. The final day on the private island was given over to relaxing and enjoying each other's company.

Assessing the Impact

"Celebrating battles won is fine, but a war won – now there is a cause for celebration!" That is how a friend of mine put it some years ago.

This chapter is about the celebration of a war won. It is now two and a half years after the formation of the board. The mid-way board meeting was held at an all hands summer picnic that the company organized as part of their participation in a local charity fundraising drive. The composition of the board has changed. Three of the original members have left – the one who was asked to resign and two who have 'rooted the pot and retired'. There are also two new seats filled. The board is up to seven members and has a very stable and productive relationship with the senior management team.

We have been through the third strategic plan review. The company is much better at it and this plan is very expansive. We are now half way through the execution o the plan and things are going very well.

Your company is now a much bigger with a highly professionalized culture and an expanded senor team. Recently they were approached by a strategic buyer. Negotiations are well under way and a liquidity event looks to be a distinct possibility. The board had turned out to be one of the major assets that had attracted the buyer in the first place.

As I sit around a table with your senior team, the conversation turns to how the board had affected each of them. You go first. *"I am a different person because of the board and members. When I look back at how I used to deal with the role of CEO, I now understand how I was limiting that was to the potential of the company. My role has changed and my understanding of leadership as well. Having these very experienced people as an on-call resource has allowed me to grow in ways I never anticipated. Letting Dr. Smith build the board was one of the best decisions I've ever made."*

Your COO is next. "*I can't believe how much my role as COO of the company had changed over time. In one way I am dealing with a much narrower remit. Lots of things that were once on my plate the business development now sees to. In another way, I am much busier than I was back then. And I spend much more time supervising others than doing the actual work.*"

Your head of business development talks about the effect that the board had on her understanding of business development. "*Before the board I saw the process as one of knocking on doors and trying to get a foot in. I was determined to make the old model work. I have kept the cards of every middle-level person that we had in the slots and last week I looked at all of them. I am amazed at the money we spent on what turned out to be dead ends. Now I have a process that I am sure works. All those business cards are just reminders of what used to be and should be no more.*"

There is no payment of any kind that can compare with helping people accomplish what they only dreamt of. The satisfaction of that time was overwhelming. These good people had met and overcome their limitations and had discovered themselves and each other in the process.

Whatever challenges came, they were ready. Whatever opportunities came before them, they were up to taking advantage of them. But most importantly, whoever they were capable of becoming, they were ready to become.

Final Thoughts

After reading the chapters I am concerned that a reader might get the impression that designing, standing up and managing an advisory board that drives corporate growth is either an easy or straightforward exercise. Before closing I want to disabuse anyone that has come to that conclusion. This much is true. My advisory boards are the single most effective way to drive a company's top line that I have ever found. Correctly done, the process can truly generate an amazing change. There is no question in my mind that the presence of five to seven highly experienced, well connected and committed senior individuals has a far greater impact on the future of a company than any other resourcing. I have watched management teams struggle with the need to up their game in anticipation of launching a board. Some have backed off of the challenge—realizing that the road is either too difficult or leads in a direction that, after reflection, they don't want to travel.

I have also helped teams come to the conclusion that, although they do want to travel those pathways, they need to take some time to prepare themselves and their company for the journey. This honorable and courageous decision has saved many from wasting precious resources and substantial negative branding.

Some management teams have tried and failed. Whether through a lack of will or potential, they were forced to the conclusion that they were not up to the challenge. But, most often, teams have faced their limitations and overcome them. They have mastered the need to reinvent themselves in order to better serve the needs of their company and compatriots. And it is these experiences that make the effort so worthwhile.

The challenge is to make business development live up to its name—to master the single most ubiquitous point of pain that any management team faces and turn it into an advantage that will allow a company to beat out its competition and become master of its future. An advisory board is the best way to do precisely that.

Contact Information

I sincerely hope that you have enjoyed this book and find it useful. You may find <u>Volume One – Forty-Six Meditations for the Thinking Chief Executive</u> - useful as well.

I am always interested to hear from readers—about their thoughts on the book or relevant war stories that relate to it. Please feel free to send either to <u>drsmith@dr-smith.com</u>.

If you are interested in exploring the possibility of building a business development team and/or an advisory board for your company, send me an e-mail. Provide me with as much information as you can. I will contact you to arrange a free consultation.

www.ingramcontent.com/pod-product-compliance
Lightning Source LLC
Chambersburg PA
CBHW051504170526
45166CB00001B/381

* 9 7 8 1 5 0 0 1 6 4 2 8 7 *